Surrealpolitik

Surreality and the National Security State

John Schoneboom

Winchester, UK
Washington, USA

JOHN HUNT PUBLISHING

First published by Zero Books, 2022
Zero Books is an imprint of John Hunt Publishing Ltd., No. 3 East St., Alresford,
Hampshire SO24 9EE, UK
office@jhpbooks.com
www.johnhuntpublishing.com
www.zero-books.net

For distributor details and how to order please visit the 'Ordering' section on our website.

Text copyright: John Schoneboom 2021

ISBN: 978 1 78535 949 1
978 1 78535 950 7 (ebook)
Library of Congress Control Number: 2021941984

A CIP catalogue record for this book is available from the British Library.

Design: Matthew Greenfield

UK: Printed and bound by CPI Group (UK) Ltd, Croydon, CR0 4YY
Printed in North America by CPI GPS partners

We operate a distinctive and ethical publishing philosophy in
all areas of our business, from our global network of authors to
production and worldwide distribution.

Contents

Acknowledgments   1
Introduction   2

Chapter 1 Dreams   10
Chapter 2 Anti-Fascism   27
Chapter 3 Paranoia   49
Chapter 4 Spectacular Crime   67
Chapter 5 Black Humor   83

Conclusion   96
Endnotes   101
References   104
Author Biography   135

Also by the Author

Fontoon. 2014, Dedalus Books. ISBN 9781909232891

We the public have become the enemy, and that is how I read Sun Tzu on the art of war today. Yet...the power of the art of deceit does not – I repeat not – necessarily weaken with exposure. Sometimes the very opposite occurs; sometimes deceit seems to thrive on exposure, as in the conjuring tricks of shamanism and in the conjuring now exercised on a global scale by the world's only superpower.

Michael Taussig, Zoology, Magic, and Surrealism in the War on Terror (2008, p. S100)

Acknowledgments

I am profoundly grateful to Andrew Crumey and Michael Green for their thoughtful feedback and helpful criticism during an academic project from which the present work grew as a sort of mutant offspring. I am also indebted to Mark Blythe, Laura Fish, David Flusfeder, and Tony Williams for their observations, questions, challenges, and encouragement along the way as I developed my lines of thought. I want to thank Jonathan Lethem for his generosity in taking the time for a lengthy conversation, which reinforced and deepened my understanding of the appropriateness of a surrealist approach in capturing the full richness of the real. You can't blame any of them for any shortcomings here, though, as any errors or misinterpretations in my subsequent adaptations of the ideas are purely my own.

I must also thank my wife and best pal Abby Schoneboom for always raising the right questions and being supportive even when she may have suspected I was some kind of lunatic, despite (or because of) my insistence on the difficulties of telling the sane from the insane while writing obsessively late into the night about paranoia, dreams, reality, and conspiracy. I'd better thank Oscar and Maisie as well, for maintaining a cheerfully surrealist atmosphere in the home and politely not noticing how groggy I might have been in the post-writing mornings as they got ready for school. I hope the packed lunches came out all right anyway.

Introduction

If you've found yourself thinking the world has gone a bit surreal lately, you're more right than you might realize. It's not just the vernacular use of the word; that is, it's not just that things are *weird*. We happen to live in a paranoid, increasingly authoritarian culture in which the real, the presumed, and the purported are indistinguishable strands of a dense hallucinatory web of mediated spectacles. In short, these times are right smack dab in the middle of actual surrealism's wheelhouse. Indeed our national-security-addled consumer-spectator society practically demands a surrealist analytical angle, albeit one that makes a distinction between the historical surrealist movement and what I will call a surrealist mode of inquiry. Let's break it down.

Consider first of all that things have gotten conspicuously unpleasant out there, since well before a certain pandemic took over the headlines. Western society would seem to be witnessing the rise of, if not textbook fascism, then something uncomfortably akin to it. What else are we to make of nominally liberal democracies characterized by total surveillance, executive kill lists, indefinite detention, authoritarian populists, militarized police, propaganda posing as journalism, shrinking civil liberties, and anti-terrorism laws being used to suppress dissent? If any of the assertions in that list strike you as unwarranted, read on; plenty of specific examples will be cited in the pages ahead.

Perhaps what we're seeing is the threat of an "inverted" form of totalitarianism, in Sheldon Wolin's terminology, dependent upon a demobilized rather than a mobilized population (2010 [2008]). Or we can follow Umberto Eco and call it an "Ur-fascism," an undercover variety, without the tell-tale black shirts (1995). We could take our cue from Herbert Böll and just call it "the era of nice monsters" (2010 [1979]).

Whatever you want to call it, these alarming tendencies coexist uneasily with the stories we tell ourselves about who we are, stories that tend to use words like "liberty" and "rights." It is, in other words, an on-the-ground reality jarringly juxtaposed against the ideals by which we persistently construct the symbolic order. Here we begin to enter surrealist territory: jarring juxtaposition, often by way of black humor, is to the technique of surrealism what anti-fascism is to its ethos. Additionally, the emergence of something-like-fascism within and alongside the persistent freedom-and-democracy political imaginary implicates the complicity of our own psychological processes at least as much as it does any externally imposed authoritarianism. As we enter the world of dreams, desires, and selective perceptions, we go even deeper into surrealist territory.

Consider what we accept without forcing an exchange of the consensual cultural self-image. Permanent war has long since been normalized. Total surveillance barely merits a shrug of indifferent shoulders, if we're not too busy actively equipping our own mobile phones with ways to track our movements, desires, and social contacts. Indefinite detention and torture now also make their bids for that state of ubiquitous invisibility. Against a backdrop of grotesque wealth inequalities, an increasingly precarious working class, militarized law enforcement, systemic racial injustice, and a certain armed segment of the US population that occasionally likes to invoke the prospect of civil war (Giglio 2020), it is difficult to imagine more perilous societal conditions. Can we address them without some kind of a reckoning with the Ur-fascist/democracy psycho-social aporia?

Welcome to the treacherous peyote desert of national security realism, a surrealist wonderland if ever there was one.

My use of the term national security realism calls back to and builds upon Mark Fisher's (2009) conception of capitalist realism as a postmodern colonization of the cultural dreamscape, a definition that already invites magnification with a surrealist lens. Capitalist realism can be understood as part of what Gilles Deleuze recognizes we have become since World War II: a "society of control" in which the "family, the school, the army, the factory are no longer the distinct analogical spaces that converge towards an owner – state or private power – but coded figures – deformable and transformable – of a single corporation that now has only stockholders" (Deleuze 1992, p. 6).

Fisher has noted that over several decades, especially in the United States, "capitalist realism has successfully installed a 'business ontology' in which it is *simply obvious* that everything in society, including healthcare and education, should be run as a business" (2009, p. 17). No less pervasive is a complementary "national security ontology" in which it is equally "obvious" that civil liberties must be sacrificed on the altar of security because of terrorists who "hate our freedoms" (Bush 2001) – a rationale not unlike that used during the Vietnam War vis-a-vis the provincial capital Bến Tre, when "it became necessary to destroy the town to save it" (Arnett 1968). This is the kind of absurd irony that practically begs to be treated with surrealist black humor. The national security ontology is the stick to the business ontology's putative carrot.

Capitalist realism is "realist" only in the sense of a resignation to perceived inevitability and lack of alternatives, with competitors and critiques either fully co-opted, as with the gestural anti-capitalism of "evil corporation" films and the barricaded impotence of permitted protest zones, or else marginalized not only right out of political discourse, but out of the collective imagination – out of our dreams. Fisher, citing Brecht, Foucault, and Badiou, notes that emancipatory politics has long understood that it "must always destroy the appearance of a 'natural order,' must reveal what is presented as necessary and inevitable to be a mere contingency" (Fisher

2009, p. 17).

As Fisher concludes, capitalist realism is so successful at absorbing and deflecting attacks and reinventing itself that the only conceivable threat to it would be if its very realism could be contested and shown to be untenable. To kick the legs out from under capitalist – or national security – realism in this way would be a Wizard of Oz moment in which we suddenly notice the small vulnerable man behind the curtain working the machinery of illusion. To lay bare the "politics of epistemic murk and the fiction of the real" promises to be what Michael Taussig described as "the true catharsis, the great counterdiscourse" (1984, p. 472) that is the political and artistic challenge of our times.

A surrealist mode of inquiry offers a political-artistic approach to the task of creatively exposing the untenability of a number of the givens of the national security ontology, which rest on grounds that are far flimsier than is generally acknowledged. It attempts to exploit what Hannah Arendt called "the curious contradiction between the totalitarian movements' avowed cynical 'realism' and their conspicuous disdain of the whole texture of reality" (1962 [1951], p. viii).

Interrogation of "general acknowledgement" is an interrogation of the "big Other": Jacques Lacan's proposition of a symbolic order or collective fiction that represents the official narrative of what can and cannot be (openly) admitted or believed in a given society.[1] The big Other is the uncritical "consumer of PR and propaganda" (Fisher 2009, p. 44-45), required to believe things that individual society members are free to reject, at least privately. It also establishes society's taboos, those areas into which the big Other is required not to venture. A surrealist mode of inquiry, always transgressive and drawn to taboos, seeks to exploit the space between what the big Other believes and what people actually accept in the privacy of their own minds.

But isn't surrealism dead? Yes and no. Certainly, the original surrealist movement rose, sustained itself, and fell in close parallel with the original fascist movement – a historical coincidence that may be more than merely curious. The same wave of zeitgeist likely carried them both; subversive impulses will wax and wane in direct proportion to repressive authority. Almost exactly a century after the publication of the first *Surrealist Manifesto* and the opening gambits of fascism, a mutated sort-of-fascism forces itself back into the conversation. How are we to understand it? How shall we reply? If the echoes of the past force us to revisit the familiar territory of old nightmares, they also invite us to confront the problem differently – to dream differently, before it's too late. I speak therefore not of resuscitating the exquisite surrealist corpse, but of adapting some of its surviving virtues in order to inform a particularly appropriate way of interrogating the incongruities and delusions of our present political condition.

Fisher has acknowledged that some of what he describes as capitalist realism could be subsumed under the rubric of postmodernism, and the same is true of some of the analytical tools and methods I attribute to surrealism. Postmodernism, after all, can fairly be described as a descendent of surrealism, with both endeavors engaged principally in the disruption of semiotic systems. One difference between the surrealists and the postmodernists is their positions regarding what Carr and Zanetti call the "nature of 'truth'" (2000, p. 904). There are different varieties of surrealist and postmodernist but, broadly speaking, the surrealists are less coy about preferring certain values over others, liberty of the imagination being chief among them. One suggested term for a post-postmodernist surrealism-plus-simulacra is hyper-surrealism (Pamatmat 2007), which has a certain appeal but may not add anything that wasn't already there. Ultimately, of course, the label is not as important as what's in the can. However, I will argue that, taken as a whole, the techniques, ethos, and preoccupations described here are most appropriately described as a *surrealist* mode of inquiry, not least because of the explicitly anti-fascist value proposition.

The stakes are high. The debasement of the notion of democracy is well underway, and a descent into a full-on police state sometimes seems only one protest crackdown away. Yet there are also positive stakes, i.e., the opportunity to "re-impassion" human life, for, as André Breton wrote in *Arcanum 17*, "Liberty is not, like liberation, a struggle against sickness, it is health" (2004 [1944], p. 128). If the assertions and assumptions of national security realism represent a kind of gaslit facade, a surrealist mode of inquiry seeks to "penetrate the veil while retaining its hallucinatory quality" (Taussig 1984, p. 471-472), the better to turn it against itself and enlarge the space of the possible. This approach amplifies what Fisher identified as the last hope of resisting the disastrous emptiness of capitalist realism.

The nexus of dreams, hyperreality, paranoia, totalitarianism, terror, art, myth, and culture is where *realpolitik* becomes *surrealpolitik.* From the foregoing I derive what I propose are the five overlapping essentials of a surrealist mode of inquiry, which will correspond to the chapters of this book:

1) Dreams: The unconscious is at the heart of surrealism and no less so for a surrealist mode of inquiry. Here we have the interplay of dream-life and conscious experience, including the full panoply of perceptual and psychological biases, as well as the dreamlike discontinuities of national security realism with its ever-shifting and contradictory lists of enemies, allies, and narratives. Here begins the search for the unreal in the real.

2) Anti-fascism: At the time of the original development of surrealism, anti-fascism was a term that could be applied more literally, but even then the ethos of the movement was more broadly conceived as a rebellion against any kind of external or internal constraint on liberty, particularly of the imagination.

For our purposes, with no interest in debates over technical definitions, we are happy simply to acknowledge that we'll be using the term as a bit of historically grounded but conveniently loose shorthand for troubling quasi-totalitarian trends, including the "internalization of boundaries that the State has put around freedom" (LaCoss 2003, p. 291) and the way the symbolic order is maintained through narrative control.

3) Paranoia: Paranoia is an often-overlooked facet of the surrealist project, but it was not only central to what Jonathan Eburne (2008) has identified as historical surrealism's 1930s *noir* period, it is at the very core of our political climate today. Conspiracy theories, commonly thought of as being the purview of a lunatic fringe, are also found in abundance in our mainstream news feeds, which, if they're not full of terrorist schemes, are unnerving us with narratives of Russian meddling or Chinese manipulation. The surrealist interest in paranoia hinges on the view-affirming selection biases and other mental processes that are as fundamental to ordinary socialization as they are to the construction of elaborate delusions, raising questions about how to tell the difference.

4) Spectacular Crime: Like paranoia, spectacular crime became a focus of surrealist interest during the 1930s noir period, although it dated back to its earliest activities, which included an avowed fascination with the Fantômas serials about a master criminal who could enter locked rooms and escape impossible situations. Using spectacular crime as a lens on morality, fear, and power, the surrealists idolized figures like the Comte de Lautréamont and the Marquis de Sade, both of whose writings pushed the limits of the laws of social acceptability. The obvious extension of this surrealist preoccupation into current times and for our own concern with national security realism is via terrorism. As a focus, terrorism comes with the added surrealist benefit of being a highly mediated form of spectacle that builds on paranoia and is inextricably bound with intelligence agency

shenanigans, narrative management, and a general "hall of mirrors" state of purported reality.

5) Black Humor: André Breton published an *Anthology of Black Humour* (2009 [1997]), making the subject part of the surrealist canon. Black humor is distinguished from other sorts of humor by its not necessarily being funny, or rather by the discomfort that arises from the juxtaposition of absurdity and horror. Freud and the unconscious are invoked here, as are rebellious impulses in this "superior revolt of the mind" (2009 [1997], p. 22). It also bears noting that, in terms of communicating ideas, few strategies are more effective than those employing humor. If nothing else, black humor helps keep everything else in this surrealist soup from being intolerably dreary.

These five mutually reinforcing signature elements provide a playful yet powerful analytical framework that is ideally suited to subjecting the assumptions of our present social condition to rigorous interrogation. Together they comprise the basis of our surrealist mode of inquiry and we will examine each of them in turn.

Chapter 1

Dreams

*Dreams, dreams, dreams, with each step the domain of dreams
expands...Dreams, dreams, dreams, nothing but dreams where the
wind wanders and barking dogs are out on the roads.*
Louis Aragon, A Wave of Dreams (2010 [1924], p. 31)

*"Well dreams, they feel real while we're in them, right? It's only when
we wake up that we realize something was actually strange. Let me ask
you a question. You never really remember the beginning of a dream,
do you? You always wind up right in the middle of what's going on.
So how did we end up here?"*
Cobb (Leonardo DiCaprio), *Inception*, 2010

Dreams and the unconscious are foundational elements of
surrealism and are, as such, a central preoccupation of the first
Surrealist Manifesto (Breton 2010 [1924]). In it, André Breton
defines "surreality" as "a kind of absolute reality" resulting
from the resolution of the two apparently contradictory states
of dreams and reality (p. 14), and questions "why should
I not grant to dreams what I occasionally refuse reality, that
is, this value of certainty in itself" (p. 12). Under this heading
of "dreams," therefore, I include not only the stories we tell
ourselves while we are asleep, but all the ways our sense of
certainty about reality – the stories we tell ourselves while we
are awake – are subject to a range of unconscious perceptual
and interpretive forces. A surrealist mode of inquiry posits a
waking world that bears more than a passing resemblance to
dreams.

What differentiates Kant, Nietzsche and Freud from the

tiresome cliché that 'life is but a dream' is the sense that the confabulations we live are consensual. The idea that the world we experience is a solipsistic delusion projected from the interior of our mind consoles rather than disturbs us, since it conforms with our infantile fantasies of omnipotence; but the thought that our so-called interiority owes its existence to a fictionalized consensus will always carry an uncanny charge. (Fisher 2009, p. 56)

The surrealist movement, for its part, overtly invoked the world of the unconscious and irrational against that of the conscious and rational, but it also suggested that what we take to be external is substantially contingent upon and subject to our inner lives – that the inner and the outer constitute a feedback loop. Leonora Carrington, for example, in *Down Below,* in relating her descent into madness as a surrealist aesthetic, described how "she and the world mirrored each other" (Hertz 2010, p. 99). Walter Benjamin credits surrealism for linking "the realization of dream elements, in the course of waking up" with a dialectical process of historical awakening (Benjamin 1999, p. 13).

When Georges Bataille, "the black surrealist of catastrophe" (Bataille 2006 [1994], p. 6), wrote that he "cannot consider someone free if they do not have the desire to sever the bonds of language within themselves" (ibid., p. 49) he was making a point not only about how language itself structures our sense of the possible, but ultimately about how severing those bonds liberates the unconscious. Here Bataille, simultaneously a sort of renegade surrealist and a strong critic of the movement, was in the midst of a passage that recognizes that "automatic writing was more than a petty provocation" because André Breton's surrealism, like poststructuralism after it, understood the sense in which reality is contingent upon language. Bataille continues:

Insubordination, if not extended to the domain of images and words, is still no more than a refusal of external forms (such as the government or the police) when ordered words and images are entrusted *to us* by a system which, one thing leading to another, causes the entirety of nature to be submitted to utility. Belief – or, rather, *servitude* to the real world – is, without the shadow of a doubt, fundamental to all servitude. (Bataille 2006 [1994], p. 49)

The imperative at the heart of surrealism to reject "servitude to the real world" is a multifaceted appeal to dreamwork. On the one hand it is a defense of the imagination, promoting the benefits of giving the freest possible rein to the unfettered, unordered, untamed mind. This is at the same time of course a recognition of the extent to which fungible reality is, individually and collectively, already a product of under-examined unconscious mechanisms, of biases and assumptions reified by language and custom. The surrealist movement associated the power of the unconscious, as via automatic writing, with the compulsion to free ourselves from bonds that may not be readily apparent.

A surrealist mode of inquiry therefore responds to André Breton's call for "a brand new laboratory where established ideas, *no matter which*, beginning with the most elementary ones, the ones most hastily exonerated, will be accepted only for purposes of study, contingent on an examination *from top to bottom* and by definition free from all preconceptions" (2004 [1944], p. 61).

The call for a surrealist mode of inquiry into the present moment in history implies an inadequacy in our usual perceptions of reality, or our usual "preconceptions." Surreality, after all, posits itself as an improvement over "ordinary" reality, begging a few questions about what reality is and what's wrong with the way we see it. It is appropriate to address these questions in the chapter on dreams because the answers, in large part, implicate the unconscious.

The heart of the idea is that what we generally take to be the facts of perceived reality are actually, to some uncertain and variable degree, fictions. They include elements that are variously constructed, edited, imposed, presumed, and incomplete. Reality is, in short, a kind of narrative spun by numerous psychological, social, and biological factors that are often, like so many narrators in fiction, unreliable. At least some of what we take to be the manifest givens of reality might therefore reflect anything from mild bias to radical illusion. As one neuroscientist (Lotto 2018) put it elegantly enough: "You never, ever see reality!"

I will refer you to neuroscientists for your neuroscience, except to borrow the proposition that what we do see in lieu of reality is a deeply personalized yet culturally conditioned neuronal representation of what our history has taught us to expect. Our senses provide us with limited, undependable, and, above all, *meaningless* information; our brains provide the meaning, based on experience and belief. It is difficult usefully to separate internal processes from external data since they form an interdependent system of reality creation; this is true of both ordinary socialization and delusion, as will be addressed in the chapter on paranoia. Of particular importance to a surrealist mode of inquiry is the phenomenon known as confirmation bias – the neophobic tendency to see only what reinforces our existing belief structures.

This focus on perception under the rubric of dreams and the unconscious forms part of the bedrock foundation of the surrealist mode of inquiry, intended to begin to chip away at our basic sense of certainty in order to expand the scope of the possible. My innovative undergraduate institution, Hampshire College, had a motto – *Non satis scire* ("to know is not enough") – that guided its own mode of inquiry. It's a good reminder that actions, not thoughts, feelings, or intentions, are what ultimately define us. A good motto for a surrealist mode of inquiry might be the détournement *Nimium scire*: to know is too much. Too-certain knowledge puts limits on new learning and imagination; contrarily, destroying assumptions frees that imagination and creates opportunities both to learn and to expand the so-called Overton Window, or the range of ideas that are conceivable within a given society.

It's not difficult to demonstrate that our perception of the world around us does not deserve our full confidence. As a personal example, I am sorry to say that I once had a very regrettable mustache. When the full horror of it finally hit me, I happened to be in a friend's bathroom. I made the arguably disgusting decision to borrow his razor and seize the moment.

As I began to shave, I got the idea that it would be funny to shave off only half the mustache. I would walk back into his living room, my friend would do a double-take, and laughter would ensue. I emerged, desperately trying not to bust out in premature guffaws at my own comic genius.

What happened instead was that several difficult-to-believe hours passed without him noticing. Over time, the undiscovered prank transformed from cheap comedy to psychological experiment. In the end I had to point it out; the only thing that ensued was awkwardness over how it was possible to miss something so glaringly obvious (and over whether it was sanitary for me to have used his razor).

The experience felt unusual, but actually the only unusual thing about it was that we became aware of the gap in perception, that we caught a glimpse of a very ordinary, very common kind of delusion. Scientists have even studied it.

The invisible gorilla experiment (Chabris and Simons 2010), more formally known as the "selective attention test," demonstrated that my friend was not uniquely oblivious. The test involves watching a video that shows a group of people passing a basketball around. Half of the players wear white, the other half wear black. Viewers are instructed to count how many times the ones in white pass the ball. As the video proceeds, a person wearing a full gorilla suit makes his way quite brazenly across the court, even pausing in the midst of all the players to beat his chest.

You'd think that would be just about impossible to miss, but surprisingly, on average half the viewers completely fail to notice the spectacle of the incongruous gorilla because they're too busy concentrating on white uniforms and counting passes. The researchers call it "inattentional blindness." I regret to report that I must count myself among those who so failed. (On the positive side, I feel like I was pretty good at counting passes.)

Any number of additional examples could be offered of commonplace illusions that implicate our senses and the way our brains process the data with which it is provided. We may see things that are not there or fail to see things that are, or we may see things bigger or smaller or longer or shorter or a different color than they really are, and, arguably, none of it matters. It's mostly trivial, in the sense that none of it puts our survival at risk (apart perhaps from the rare real gorilla that we fail to notice in time).

Yet it's worth pondering whether mental processes similar to those that have us seeing religious symbols on a piece of burnt toast might affect a range of other interpretations we impose on the world. In fact, if you pursue the subject with the least amount of rigor, you're soon forced to admit not only that your world-image is hopelessly subjective, distorted, and incomplete, but also that you fundamentally have no idea what reality even is or whether it's a concept that has meaning. After all, before we even get to our conscious and unconscious biases, we are privy only to the tiny sliver of the universe that we've evolved to perceive, a proportion that is not only minuscule compared to what actually exists, but that is paltry even compared to the sense-data registered by a below-average dog. And that's if the whole thing isn't just an elaborate computer simulation fed into a brain in a jar.

Observations of our human limitations don't have much practical use since, comfortingly, we're all more or less in the same boat. When we speak of reality we implicitly speak of the slice that counts "for us" or ultimately "for me." But this baseline awareness of our dependence upon potentially deceptive cognitive processes lays the groundwork upon which we can add layers of biases, assumptions, beliefs, and mistakes. Or rather, it begins the process of chipping away at the groundwork upon which the rest of our misapprehensions are laid.

Some illusions usefully reveal the extent to which our perceptions depend on our beliefs and assumptions, or in other words on our mental models of the world. The beliefs and assumptions from which we construct our mental models inevitably comprise conscious and unconscious, true and false, tested and untested elements.

Jan Westerhoff (2010) offers the example of the moon stubbornly appearing larger when it is near the horizon than when it is high in the sky. Measurement demonstrates that it is not so: a ruler held at arm's length will show the moon is the same width regardless. The sky, in Westerhoff's explanation, is felt instinctively to be like an inverted shallow soup bowl, such that the edges of the horizon are felt to be further away than the middle. Our minds put together intuited-further-distance and same-raw-size to give us the impression of "bigger" at the horizon. It's the same thing our minds do when presented with, for example, a distant basketball and a close-up tennis ball. They may appear at face value to have the same diameter, but our minds "do the math" for us and we'll still see – or, perhaps more accurately, feel – the basketball as larger.

Few of us would consciously accept the notion that the sky

is like a shallow bowl, but many of us see that moon as larger anyway. The key meaning here for our purposes is simply that "beliefs do not have to be explicit" (Westerhoff 2010, p. 40) in order to affect our perceptions. The unconscious has real effects on how we see the world, both literally and figuratively. The same process that works to give us an accurate picture of tennis balls and basketballs works to give us a false impression of the moon.

The role of the unconscious is what links perception and bias to a surrealist mode of inquiry. Recognition of the unconscious interpretive machinery of perception raises questions about how our experiences of reality are conditioned in ways of which we are not often aware. To what extent might all our perceptions of everything from urban environments to large-scale political events be similarly contingent upon obscure transactions among our beliefs, myths, ideologies, and misdirected attentions? If we can effectively project our expectations onto the external world, it is reasonable to wonder how much of reality is conjured like dreams by our unconscious minds. How many mustaches aren't really there? How many beliefs are just products of confirmation bias? How many things look like nails just because we think like a hammer? These are thoughts that exist in tension with the idea that we live in a rational age of science and reason. This tension is among the factors that gave rise to the surrealist movement in the first place, and it leads us to our next step.

The suspicion that our understanding of reality relies upon more than just the conscious and logical parts of our brains is not the only blow to the supposed age of reason. There is another suspicion, shared by surrealism and critical theory: that post-Enlightenment instrumental rationality is a dangerously narrow and misleading construct anyway. For all the liberating power of science over superstition, for example, there is also a sense that the same thinking that devalues myth leads to a loss of meaning and values, and to an impoverishment of life by a perspective skewed toward the utilitarian.

If the ways and means of life are to be judged in terms of use-value, the question of whose ends are to be served is raised. Horkheimer and Adorno's (2002 [1944], p. 16) observation that "[p]ower confronts the individual as the universal, as the reason which informs reality" is amplified by Breton's identification of "the 'reign of logic' as the principal means employed to suppress the imagination's innate rebelliousness" (LaCoss and Spiteri 2003, p. 7). One of our critical tasks, then, is to expose the web of assumptions and contingencies that pose as ontological givens as no more than what Foucault called "a thing of sand" (2001, p. 34).

The surrealist resistance to the tyranny of narrowly instrumental reasoning – perhaps the most fundamental element of resistance to capitalist realism – begins as an opportunity for an individual's private mental processes. Herbert Marcuse noted the phenomenon of the "absorption of ideology into reality" (1991 [1964], p. 11); he was also among those who linked Breton's movement to Frankfurt School thought, arguing that "the surrealistic effort...is more than a mere enlargement of our perception, imagination, reason...[it is also intended] to undo the mutilation of our faculties by the established society and its requirements" (Rosemont 1989a, p. 40).

The surrealist mode of inquiry in this sense can be described as the inverse of the notion of getting a grip on reality; it is an effort to break reality's grip on us. This effort does not, however, imply a wholesale rejection of rationality. Indeed it can be described as an attempt to improve rationality rather than to discard it. This is precisely why surreality for Breton was not a distorted or warped reality but an undistorted and unwarped one, in which the French prefix "sur" implies a superior conception of reality. What could be more rational than critiquing rationality? As Baudrillard (2008, p. 14) asked: "Is there anything but a *discourse* of the real and the rational?"

Thus far, applying these observations to a surrealist mode of inquiry, we have perhaps not much more than a base-level awareness that our perception of reality is, to some degree, a construction of our own biases and assumptions, and that we might exercise our imaginations to conjure a larger set of possibilities – a new reality. This is useful. But there is an additional element of dreams that is particularly suitable to informing a surrealist mode of inquiry relevant to the national security state, and that is the notion of discontinuity.

In dreams, the discontinuous is the norm and usually arouses no particular sense of the uncanny. One moment we are lost in an unknown part of the city, the next moment in a house strangely reminiscent of our childhood home, and the next moment in some remote café with terrible anxiety that we've completely forgotten to pick up the children from school. At no time, as Leonardo DiCaprio's character Cobb notes in Christopher Nolan's film *Inception*, do we ever think to ask how we got there. Dream reality is infinitely plastic, sustains any number of contradictions, and is perpetually renegotiable.

The national security state is the same.

In the hall of mirrors that is intelligence agencies, terrorism, counterterrorism, and war, landscapes shift suddenly, allies become enemies, and the dead can live to fight another day, all without rupturing the bubble of the dreamlike narrative. If it were merely shifting alliances of convenience according to the exigencies of the geopolitical moment – the United States becoming cordial with Saddam Hussein when both had designs against Iran – that would be ordinary realpolitik. When the US military suddenly admits that a notorious terrorist, on the other hand, was a fictional character all along – *and then he continues to be in the news anyway* – that is something else again. That is surrealpolitik.

Abu Omar Al Baghdadi was one of the world's most famous terrorists. He was the head of the Islamic State of Iraq, also known as Al Qaeda in Iraq, the precursor organization to ISIS. In 2007, he was reported captured twice in March (Semple 2007) and killed in May (Cave 2007). To be sure, his identity in those instances was later disputed. In July, the US military declared he had been a fictional character all along and identified the elderly voice actor who "played" him (Gordon 2007). Notionally, Al Qaeda in Iraq had itself invented him, in order to put an Iraqi face on what the Americans said was really a foreign insurgency. In any case, by November he was back in *The New York Times*, calling for attacks against local leaders aligned with the United States (Buckley 2007), with nary a mention of the fictionality that had been so boldly declared in the pages of that same newspaper only 4 months earlier.

A year later, in November 2008, he was in the news once again as a straightforwardly really existing person, having issued a 25-minute audiotaped speech as part of a "psychological duel" with the United States (Slackman and Mekhennet 2008). In April 2009, he was reported captured by Iraqi officials, although a "spokesman for the United States military, which has suggested that he might not exist, said Tuesday that the military could still not confirm his arrest" (Dagher and Kakan 2009). Finally, in April 2010, he was killed for the last time and, contrary to earlier reports that he had been invented to put an Iraqi face on the insurgency's foreign leadership, was revealed to be an actual Iraqi whose real name was Hamid Dawud Muhammad Khalil al-Zawi, and who used Abu Omar Al Baghdadi as his *nom de guerre* (Myers 2010).

Killed, captured, killed again, real, fictional, real again, Iraqi, not Iraqi – as in a dream, none of these contradictory sequential narratives get questioned, explained, or reconciled. New realities simply supersede old incompatible ones and we shift with them, gently down the stream. It can perhaps all be chalked up to the fog of war and what, after all, is more dreamlike than fog?

It should be becoming clear, if it wasn't already, how the elements of spectacular crime and paranoia have a mutually reinforcing relationship with the element of dreamwork in a surrealist mode of inquiry, particularly with reference to the national security state. Once we become aware that the fabric of a narrative has worn thin from repeated wear, the distinctions between reality and delusion become less clear and we enter the realm of paranoia. Which story are we to believe? The most recent one, by virtue of what, its most-recentness, its thus-far-unsupersededness? With how much certainty? For how long? Where, ultimately, is the foundation for our belief? "It isn't here," as Ingrid Bergman's character in *Gaslight* (Cukor 1944) said. "You must have dreamed you put it there."

The Al Baghdadi story is far from unique in the complicated world of terrorism and counterterrorism, and other similar examples will be explored in the chapter on spectacular crime. There is one other example worth touching on under the rubric of dreams, however, and that is the case of Abu Musab al-Zarqawi: al Baghdadi's predecessor as leader of Al Qaeda in Iraq.

A key moment in establishing Zarqawi's position in this regard occurred in February 2004, when a letter ostensibly written by him was leaked to *New York Times* reporter Dexter Filkins. In the letter, Zarqawi boasts of his own importance and declares Al Qaeda's intention to foment sectarian violence throughout Iraq. Filkins' article (2004) expressed none of the doubts that he later claimed to have had about the document's authenticity (Ricks 2006). The story rapidly circulated around the newspapers of the world, giving President George W. Bush a much-needed boost to his tenuous claim of a linkage between Iraq and Al Qaeda. By later in the year, however, *The Telegraph* was reporting that the letter was "almost certainly a hoax" (Blomfield 2004), and by 2 years later the US military had acknowledged that the fake document was part of its own "propaganda campaign" to "magnify" Zarqawi's "very small part" in the insurgency (Ricks 2006). From public enemy number one to virtual non-entity, just like that. All that stuff – years' worth – about the dastardly leader of the terrible organization? Never mind. Or still consider him the terrorist leader. Either way. Whatever.

What has any of this to do with dreams? Apart from the aforementioned discontinuity of the reality-dream edit, the answer lies too in the art of propaganda, as elucidated by one of its foremost proponents: Sigmund Freud's nephew, Edward Bernays. Even by the time Bernays wrote his seminal work on the topic (2005 [1928]), the term propaganda had taken on pejorative connotations, and for good reason (Ponsonby's *Falsehood in War Time* (2005 [1928]) was released the same year). While acknowledging that in the wrong hands the power of propaganda could be a force for ill, Bernays argued for a more benign interpretation, whereby it was a neutral and inevitable tool that was indispensable in organizing the masses toward socially beneficial ends.

Bernays was evidently a principled man himself – when the ill effects of smoking became undeniable, he not only quit working for the tobacco industry but actively worked against disinformation in cigarette sales (Bernays 2005 [1928], p. 25) – but even his best attempts to put a sanguine face on his art had sinister undertones. He described propaganda as "the conscious and intelligent manipulation of the organized habits and opinions of the masses" by "an invisible government which is the true ruling power of our country" (p. 37). This aspect of propaganda will be discussed further in the chapter on anti-fascism. For the present purposes of this discussion of dreams, it is noteworthy that Bernays' analysis is replete with Freud-influenced references to subconscious associations, the "group mind," "the mental clichés and the emotional habits of the public," and ways to elicit predictable reactions with manipulative stimuli aimed at a "sensitive spot." The ultimate goal of the whole exercise is "regimenting the public mind every bit as much as an army regiments the bodies of its soldiers" (p. 52).

Surrealism, of course, was developing at precisely the same time and responding to the same heady mixture of Freudianism and a kind of traumatized euphoria in the aftermath of the First World War. Both surrealists and propagandists strove to influence public opinion, both in part by exploiting the unconscious. Obviously enough, surrealism represents in many ways the very conceptual opposite of propaganda, with a goal of un-regimenting the public mind (making the eventual cooptation of surrealist art as propaganda in advertising a bit of a cruel irony). Surrealism also dealt with minds one at a time, whereas propaganda deals in masses of them. Generally speaking, it might be said that, from a common interest in the unconscious, propaganda seeks to create order from chaos; surrealism seeks something like the reverse.

The two worlds collided in the person of Marcel Mariën, a Belgian surrealist who happened to work in the field of propaganda as a public relations specialist. His presumably facetious "Théorie de la révolution mondiale immediate" (theory of immediate world revolution) involved the creation of two spurious political parties, the Imaginary Party and the Counter Party, who would secretly share the same headquarters. They would have two facets: one public and legal, the other secret and illegal. They would stage campaigns based on a thorough understanding of propaganda techniques, and between the two of them secure a parliamentary mandate. The secret headquarters, run by a tiny number of elite representatives, would be funded by crime and terrorism: real or implied violence directed against bank managers, preferably involving flamethrowers. Ultimately, the secret common headquarters would be revealed in order to provide a psychological shock, disrupting unconscious associations and stimulating a spontaneous revolution by people lulled into and then woken up from a dream.

The juxtaposition of the preposterous and the mundane, so unexpectedly common in life as it is in art, forces an uneasy mapping of reality in our minds. We must sustain two realities simultaneously, one comfortably familiar, the other absurd, dangerous, and difficult to reconcile. On the one hand, we accept the latter by dismissing it, the same way we might filter out uncomfortable realities like homeless people rattling cups of change on the high street. At the same time, however, one feels just below the surface that the ordinary is fragile and is hiding something. Tension arises from repeated breaches of the ordinary by the strange, and from the subsequent attempts to ignore or repair the damage. What is striking is how much strangeness reality can accommodate, or how determined people are to pretend that things are normal. This is dreamwork.

Jonathan Lethem's novels are overwhelmingly about this phenomenon, the uneasy coexistence of the ordinary with the uncanny. In his own words it is one of his "obsessive subjects, [the idea] that we're editing and creating amnesiac narratives to survive all the time" (Lethem 2015). Reality is like a bubble in that it can be devastated by a sudden rupture, but our psychology is such that it also reseals as instantly as it bursts. So there's a constant tension, we do notice things that don't fit the script, things that jar us into a momentary awareness of absurdity or the sense of a falseness, a simulated quality, glimpses behind the scenes, but in the flow of life we ignore, we forget, we pretend, we shrug off. We create an "amnesiac narrative" to avoid uncomfortable issues and difficult questions or just to cope with getting through the day. There's a personal and social inertia that keeps us going, with no time to dwell on the oddities or explore the puzzles. Even so, there's just no getting around that in life as in art, a "realism" that excludes the uncanny, the dreamlike discontinuities, the irrational, the hidden, the aporia, is not real at all. These things are all around us, no matter how much we normally try not to look at them. A surrealist mode of inquiry insists that we embrace them, front and center.

For a surrealist mode of inquiry, the blurriest margins of these territories – between real and unreal, conscious and unconscious, sane and insane – are where things are most interesting, where the stakes are highest, and where we can most fruitfully query the reliability of our most trusted assumptions.

Let us conclude this chapter by noting Jim Garrison's twist on the phrase "American dream." Garrison, the District Attorney for New Orleans, discussed his experience investigating the assassination of John F. Kennedy in an interview with *Playboy* magazine (Norden 1967). The interview brings together most of the strands of a surrealist mode of inquiry in one place with specific reference to the national security state: dreams, anti-fascism, spectacular crime, and paranoia. All that's missing is the black humor. His comments are worth quoting at some length:

> What worries me deeply, and I have seen it exemplified in this case, is that we in America are in great danger of slowly evolving into a proto-fascist state...Of course, you can't spot this trend to fascism by casually looking around. You can't look for such familiar signs as the swastika, because they won't be there...But this isn't the test. The test is: What happens to the individual who dissents? In Nazi Germany, he was physically destroyed; here, the process is more subtle, but the end results can be the same...I've learned enough about the machinations of the CIA in the past year to know that this is no longer the dreamworld America I once believed in...I'm afraid, based on my own experience, that fascism will come to America in the name of national security.

This is the question that a surrealist mode of inquiry is so well suited to addressing. Which is closer to reality – the American Dream, or Garrison's "dreamworld America"?

Chapter 2

Anti-Fascism

How to persuade the reader that the actual direction of contemporary politics is toward a political system the very opposite of what the political leadership, the mass media, and think tank oracles claim that it is, the world's foremost exemplar of democracy?
Sheldon Wolin, Democracy Inc. (2010 [2008], p. xx)

How times have changed. A decade after the Vietnam War ended, it was still possible to persuade voters that a former member of a covert torture and assassination program wasn't suitable to be a state's chief law enforcement officer. Since 9/11, it has become a badge of honor.
Douglas Valentine, The CIA as Organized Crime (2017, p. 276)

Historical surrealism was explicitly anti-fascist (Eburne 2008), which, in tandem with the current tension between national security excesses and civil liberties, accounts for its inclusion as integral to a surrealist mode of inquiry. If we're going to bandy the term fascism about today without waltzing blithely into hyperbole, a few questions are begged. What does the term mean in a current context? How strict a definition is too strict? How loose is too loose? To what and to whom might we apply it? A good fundamental question is one asked by André Breton, pondering Hitler's version in *Arcanum 17* (2004 [1944], p. 27): "Is it true, or rather will it be certain tomorrow that this error is particularly, exclusively German?" Today, surveying the political landscape at home, are we seeing a few excesses within an otherwise sound system, or is there something more to worry about?

Wolin's question about persuasion, quoted above, suggests the problem might be not only ominous, but also in some sense hidden. His question is as strange as it is essential. One could be forgiven for presuming that people heading into fascist-like conditions would be the last ones needing to be persuaded of that fact. Yet Wolin's implication is that the task is anything but straightforward if the entirety of that reader's social conditioning has been dedicated to marginalizing such notions as preposterous, as literally inconceivable.

This concern with the unimaginable is a hallmark of surrealist anti-fascism. It is the question of dreaminess, an extension of the unconscious perceptual and interpretive mechanisms from the previous chapter that, particularly in combination with effective propaganda, can have us living inside the projection of a misleading image that obscures an uncomfortable separate reality. Yet were this the case, it would not come without tensions, stresses, ruptures. If the symbolic order – the big Other – excludes the possibility of fascism, what happens when fascism nonetheless appears?

One possible explanation for Wolin's difficulty in persuasion might simply be that his implication is in fact false or overstated: that the symbolic order has substantial integrity in this regard and the political system is genuinely an approximate exemplar of liberal values. In this view, fascism really is mutually exclusive with democracy; it is something that we fight, something that happens to other people. The alternative – that the proposition is true, that the symbolic order is a hypnotic veil, that the work of propagandists has had a profound mystifying effect on public perceptions, that we enter into tentative negotiations with paranoia – is the notion that a surrealist mode of inquiry engages vis-a-vis the national security state. One need not end with the conclusion that a fascist shift is real, in a surrealist mode of inquiry, but one must not begin with the conclusion that it is impossible.

Buckle your seatbelts: this chapter will take us on a whirlwind tour of disparate but related trends in US and UK society – government, media, technology – the purpose of which is to examine whether a concern with anti-fascism is justified today. It may at times feel a bit like the stream of consciousness of surrealist automatic writing, but each twist and turn we will take is grounded in a single notion: the suppression of dissent, whether by the punishment of brutality and the loss of civil rights or by the persuasions and exclusions of narrative management.

Fascism is a tendentious word that – not unlike the word surrealism – has been devalued both by imprecise vernacular usage and by overly specific technical criteria. Probably the most common domestic usage of the F word at present is with reference to alt-right extremist groups whose signature characteristics include racism, xenophobia, and a fetishistic obsession with guns. For those of us who do not enjoy membership of such groups, it's straightforwardly non-controversial to point the fascism finger in this direction. For our purposes, however, as long as these groups maintain an "outsider" status, no matter how disagreeable or dangerous they might be, by definition they pose no challenge to the theoretical integrity of the symbolic order; society's official narrative has no trouble condemning neo-Nazis as emphatically as you please.[1]

A surrealist mode of inquiry adds nothing to the platitudinous observation that swastika-waving chest-beaters exhibit fascist tendencies, so, with its nose for the tabooed and the transgressive, it seeks instead the more insidious forms. In this context the primary purpose of a surrealist mode of inquiry is precisely to investigate the extent to which the symbolic order provides cover for that which it purports to oppose. The stakes go beyond mere hypocrisy on the part of individuals or even an elite class. At stake is the symbolic order itself.

Against this background, anti-fascism should here be understood as a convenient shorthand for a broader surrealist impulse against the systematic repression of thought, expression, and action under authoritarian societies of control. In the context of Mark Fisher's notion of capitalist realism, the surrealist declaration in *Liberté est un mot Vietnamien* is pertinent: "[C]apitalism has abused that noblest of key words – 'freedom' – ...with the intent to secure total control...Surrealism only has meaning so long as it stands against...the implementation of a new totalitarianism" (LaCoss 2003, p. 288).

This broader sense of the term is what Umberto Eco has called Ur-Fascism. Eco notes that fascism has a "fuzziness" that allows it to take many forms, adding or shedding particular qualities but maintaining a "family resemblance":

> We must keep alert, so that the sense of these words will not be forgotten again. Ur-Fascism is still around us, sometimes in plainclothes. It would be so much easier, for us, if there appeared on the world scene somebody saying, "I want to reopen Auschwitz, I want the Black Shirts to parade again in the Italian squares." Life is not that simple. Ur-Fascism can come back under the most innocent of disguises. Our duty is to uncover it and to point our finger at any of its new instances – every day, in every part of the world. (Eco 1995)

Where does legitimate counterterrorism end, for example, and fuzzy Ur-Fascism begin? Fisher has noted how capitalist realism maintains its claim to realism in part because it has been able to deflect and coopt challenges. National security realism survives exposure of its excesses in a similar way. A bit of torture (Lewis 2014), the murder of a journalist or two (Daley 2020) – these may attract critical attention but ultimately, if denial fails, they can be passed off as anomalies, mistakes, or regrettable-but-necessary measures in an ugly, dangerous world. The body of critics may grow and the big Other's security narrative may be tarnished or forced to adapt, but as long as the damage remains below some unknown critical threshold, the narrative survives without an appreciable loss of fundamental legitimacy.

Ultimately, in any case, if a goal of a surrealist mode of inquiry is to deny security realism's purchase on the real, the task is incomplete if it considers only the mechanisms of coercion and fear and neglects desire and delusion – the complicity of our psychological processes. Terror, desire, and delusion will be considered in more depth in the overlapping chapters on spectacular crime and paranoia. Under the rubric of the present chapter, we will limit ourselves to a brief, if circuitous, exploration of the liminal terrain between security and fascism.

At the risk of stating the obvious, an authoritarian surveillance state mentality has already done a great deal of violence to civil liberties in the United States. The issues themselves are no secret. They are not so much hidden as obscured by a combination of factors that allow them to remain unrecognized, plausibly denied, or sufficiently excused by the persistence of national security realism.

As individual issues, even in the form of a steady drip, they lose much of their power to alarm. Indeed, we become inured to them. They become normalized, albeit in tension with our collective self-image. Assembled together, however, and presented as a cultural tapestry, the effect is somewhat more jarring: we have a literal permanent state of emergency (Paye 2006) featuring a global war on terror, i.e., a war of dubious legality against a poorly defined abstract concept with no geographical constraints and no prospect of victory, defeat, or conclusion (Murray 2011; Sanders 2011; Spinney 2011; Bacevich 2013; Stanford 2015); total surveillance, in which all communications are monitored and our own devices used to watch and listen to us (Simons and Spafford 2003; Miller 2014; Sylvain 2014; Ganguly 2015; David 2017); militarized domestic police forces with broad powers over our lives, liberties, and property, using SWAT team tactics with impunity even against those suspected only of nonviolent crimes (Schaefer 2002; Wolf 2007; Whitehead 2013; Alexander and Myers-Montgomery 2016; Bolduc 2016; Sack 2017); centralized corporate media that (for a variety of reasons) fail to contest government narratives (Chomsky and Herman 2002 [1988]; Borjesson 2004 [2002]; Davies 2009); protest and dissent being treated under legal provisions for terrorism (Fang 2015; Levin 2017; ACLU undated-a); and a loss of civil liberties to the extent that US citizens, like everyone else, can now be declared enemy combatants by arbitrary executive decree and be indefinitely detained or killed without recourse to due process (Friedersdorf 2012; Sarah 2013; Georgeanne A 2014; Diab 2015; Gee 2015; Powell 2016).

It's easy enough to identify abuses of power and repressive measures, and to note the ironies of repression-in-the-name-of-freedom. Indeed what quickly becomes remarkable is the resilience of the symbolic order in the face of so many damaging inconsistencies. The absurdities and contradictions are certainly in themselves a magnet for a surrealist approach, but such laundry lists alone, while necessary, do not appear to be sufficient to take the real out of national security realism. It's almost as if, once we excuse one or two or ten such instances, any number can be added without making much of an impression; they are pre-excused; we've heard it all before.

What the weight of the assembled abuses does do is beg the question that a surrealist mode of inquiry is built to investigate: how much fascism is too much? If adding more damning data doesn't appear to be an effective way of answering that question before it's too late, then perhaps altering the framework of perception is the more useful way to proceed.

The point, for a surrealist mode of inquiry, is not to get bogged down in terminology and decide whether the US (or the UK) is an "emerging police state"[2] (Whitehead 2013), or is undergoing a "fascist shift"[3] (Wolf 2007), or represents "inverted totalitarianism"[4] (Wolin 2010 [2008]). The narrowing of civil liberties is self-evident, regardless of what we think about it or what we call it. If the "what" of what's happening to our civil liberties is obvious enough, the "why" is considerably less so.

There is a spectrum of explanatory possibilities. On one end is the story told by the big Other: the authoritarian narrowing of civil liberties is an unfortunate yet inevitable result of a well-meaning and necessary national security regime; we are trading some of our rights to achieve a greater degree of safety. A bit further along the spectrum we might add: abuses and mistakes occur above and beyond the necessary and intended, but these artifacts of overzealousness do not compromise the fundamental legitimacy of the system; the big Other regrets any inconvenience.

Even further along we might have: the legitimacy of the national security system has been compromised by authoritarian opportunists who have hijacked some of its well-intentioned provisions for political purposes such as stifling dissent.

At the far end: the authoritarian narrowing of civil liberties has nothing to do with national security and everything to do with protection of privileged elites from the threat of unruly masses; the so-called national security regime is primarily intended to maintain order and stifle dissent both at home and abroad, probably because unrest is expected from the combination of increasingly grotesque wealth inequalities and increasingly scarce natural resources; the big Other's story is a tissue of lies from top to bottom; and things are going to get much, much worse.

It's not too difficult to see how the elements of anti-fascism and paranoia generously overlap here, yet one need not leap to the far end of the spectrum in order to subject the symbolic order to the stress test of a surrealist mode of inquiry. It's difficult to know where to begin and end with a brief sketch of a broad area – abuses of the national security regime – about which many books and even more lengthy articles have been written. But in our search for the why of the modern national security state, we shall focus on the disconnect between its theory and its practice. One reasonable starting point is with the USA PATRIOT Act, hereafter referred to more quietly in lower case as the Patriot Act.[5]

The core provisions at least of the Patriot Act had been written by 1995, in the Omnibus Counterterrorism Act introduced by Joe Biden, which at that time did not have enough support for a vote (US Senate 1995). Immediately following the attacks of September 11, 2001, the Patriot Act was signed into law with a minimum of debate, introducing long-desired surveillance powers that, according to the American Civil Liberties Union (ACLU), "fundamentally altered the relationship Americans share with their government" (2009, p. 7). Under Section 215, the Act allowed for secret court orders to enable the FBI to seize "any tangible thing" – from credit card purchases to internet browsing history – from anyone, without their knowledge. The order also comes with a "gag," so the recipient who must turn over the data is prohibited from ever telling anyone that it happened (Timm 2011).

National Security Letters (NSLs) already allowed the FBI to do the same thing without a court order, but the Act lowered the standards for issuing an NSL so that people without direct links to terrorism or spies – and without evidence or suspicion of wrongdoing – can be subjected to one. Of 192,000 NSLs issued between 2003 and 2006, only one was related to a terrorism conviction, and in that case the conviction would have happened anyway (ACLU undated-c).

The ACLU concludes that "there is little evidence that the Patriot Act has been effective in making America more secure from terrorists" but that there is abundant evidence "that the government abused these authorities in ways that...violate the rights of innocent people" (2009). The Electronic Frontier Foundation (EFF), having evaluated the results of its numerous

Freedom of Information Act (FOIA) requests, reached a similar conclusion, that "it's crystal clear that the 'emergency' measure sold as a necessary step in the fight against terrorism is being used routinely to violate the privacy of regular people in non-terrorism cases" (Timm 2011).

Senator Ron Wyden of Utah, who was privy to classified information, confirms the accuracy of these judgments. Wyden has made a distinction between the official Patriot Act – the one you can look up on Wikipedia or read about in official documents – and "the real Patriot Act, the secret interpretation of the law that the government is actually relying upon" (Sadowski 2013). He has further stated that when (or if) people find out about these secret interpretations "they are going to be stunned and they are going to be angry" (Savage 2011).

Anti-terrorism authority has been wielded far more often against non-terrorists than against terrorists. Sometimes other illegal activity is caught – Patriot Act provisions have led to charges for money laundering, fraud, drug possession, and immigration offenses (ACLU undated-c) – and sometimes the authority is used against legal, peaceful dissent. The FBI has opened "domestic terrorism" surveillance operations on civil rights groups advocating for racial justice and immigrants' rights (Levin 2019); police have gone undercover to infiltrate and spy on anti-fracking activists (Fang and Horn 2016); the FBI Joint Terrorism Task Force tracked Black Lives Matters activists (Fang 2015), indigenous protesters and environmentalists at Standing Rock (Levin 2017), quite a few other "peaceful advocacy groups" (ACLU undated-b), and, apparently unsuccessfully, tried to infiltrate at least one vegan pot luck dinner (Snyders 2008).

The line between government and corporate interests is blurred, if not erased, in some of these operations. The FBI and the Department of Homeland Security worked hand in hand with the big banks in their surveillance and violent crackdown on the

Occupy Wall Street activists (Wolf 2012). Movements opposed to the Dakota Access Pipeline also attracted the surveillance, infiltration, and counterterrorism interest of TigerSwan, "a shadowy international mercenary and security firm" working on behalf of the pipeline corporation and collaborating with police departments of "at least five states" (Brown, Parrish et al. 2017).

But if you thought the Patriot Act was bad, the revelations that came courtesy of whistleblower Edward Snowden render it almost quaint by comparison. It turns out the FBI's targeting of thousands of innocent people is dwarfed by the 20 *trillion* transactions – counting only phone calls and emails (Greenwald 2013) – captured by the National Security Agency (NSA). The NSA literally tries to "collect it all" – every telephone call, every internet interaction, "all forms of electronic communication... on the earth" (ibid.) – for storage in a massive Utah facility that can absorb the data equivalent of the contents of the Library of Congress every minute of every day for "hundreds of years" (Carroll 2013). As journalist Glenn Greenwald notes (2013), this is the very "definition of the ubiquitous surveillance state."

None of this is to suggest that law enforcement ought not to worry about actual home-grown extremism, which demonstrably exists and is certainly worrisome. But if the cure does more damage to democracy and its values than the disease, one is forced to wonder about the doctor's motivations.

On January 6, 2021, a so-called "Stop the Steal" protest in Washington DC turned ugly when a group of Donald Trump supporters entered the Capitol Building and violence ensued. The event was widely characterized as an insurrection or a coup attempt, and talk of domestic terrorism, already *au courant*, reached an almost frenzied pitch. Incoming president Joe Biden, who frequently boasts of having authored the Patriot Act and has referred to its provisions as "measured and prudent" (US Senate 2001), promised to make a priority of enacting a new domestic terrorism act (Levy 2021) likely to exacerbate the already widely abused Patriot Act provisions (Savage 2021). Within 3 weeks of the January 6 event, nine states had introduced 14 anti-protest bills, provisions of which included criminalizing participation in disruptive protests, preventing demonstrators from receiving benefits or government jobs, and "offering legal protections to those who shoot or run over protesters" (Brown and Lacy 2021).

It's not just the United States. The United Kingdom is using similar tactics and raising similar concerns. At the time of this writing, a strange new police bill lumping protests in with knifings and crimes against children has been proposed by the Boris Johnson government, and is expected to have "a hugely detrimental effect on civil liberties" in the UK (Allegretti and Wolfe-Robinson 2021). The draconian approach to dissent may be getting worse, but is not new. Anti-terrorism powers were used to "deal robustly" with climate change protesters at Heathrow Airport (Vidal and Pidd 2007). A parliamentary report expressed concern that "laws intended for counter-terrorism are being misused in an increasingly heavy-handed approach to policing protests" (Hirsch 2009). The "Stansted 15," activists who blocked migrant deportations, were convicted on terrorism charges, although those convictions were later overturned by a judge who feared it set a bad precedent against nonviolent protest (Nathanson 2021). The Snowden documents reveal that the Government Communications Headquarters (GCHQ) engages in practices similar to those of the NSA, collecting information from "every visible user on the internet" (Morris 2015) in addition to engaging in operations intended "to foster 'obedience' and 'conformity'" (Greenwald and Fishman 2015a).

Intelligence agency interest in obedience and conformity raises a host of other issues that are pertinent to our discussion of dissent in relation to our putative quasi-fascism. Of particular interest to a surrealist mode of inquiry is the state of tension maintained in the nexus of misinformation, disinformation, dissent, debate, and censorship. The symbolic order or big Other didn't come from nowhere and it is not maintained magically. Narratives require storytellers. Those with privileged narrative-driving power – authorities and their proxies, corporate media, key influencers – must deal not only with telling stories but with hecklers. They must deal with dissent, and in ways the pre-internet institutions did not have to worry about.

The advent of the online networked world has provided avenues for independent investigative journalism, whistleblowers, and push-back on official narratives to which the establishment is beginning to respond in earnest. A surrealist mode of inquiry actively seeks locations of tension in which information is maligned not because it is harmful to the public interest, but because it is harmful to the symbolic order. When dissent is "debunked" as misinformation or disinformation, who fact-checks the fact-checkers?

The public discourse on disinformation does not tend to focus on the journalistic failures of the *Washington Post* or the *New York Times* to contest the narrative of weapons of mass destruction (WMDs) in Iraq or other important stories through the years that turned out to be untrue. In fact it's not just the odd massive mistake; mainstream journalism has structural issues – various economic, social, and political pressures and influences – that render it replete with "flat earth news" – stories that are "widely believed and devoid of reality" (Davies 2009, p. 111) – to deeply distorting effect.

What has been created is a vortex of concentric forces, reducing reality to a small cluster of reports, flowing through a handful of monopoly providers who, in turn, channel each other's stories into their own streams. Frequently unchecked, commonly created by PR, this consensus account of the world is inherently inadequate in its selection of stories, inherently unreliable in its reporting, daily generating the mass production of ignorance. (Davies 2009, p. 108)

Although the reality-twisting power of these main narrative-driving engines of the symbolic order – with the power to start wars and affect the global economy – is incomparably greater than the relatively puny independent alternative media, the main targets of official anti-disinformation efforts are always the latter – the places where voices are most likely to stray off the reservation. These efforts are always designed around discrediting sources rather than promoting critical thinking – they typically provide lists of sites to avoid because they're full of "Russian propaganda." PropOrNot (2016) infamously published such a list, boosted by the *Washington Post* despite its obvious flaws, its "reckless and unproven allegations," and its "outright defamation [of]...obviously legitimate news sites" (Norton and Greenwald 2016).

In the post-WMD era, it's impossible to miss the irony of the glass house *Washington Post* throwing stones at the independent media. The best defense of the corporate media in this regard would be to note that any news source will get some things wrong some of the time. Following the logic of this clearly true observation would seem to indicate that the best way, indeed the only way, to evaluate the credibility of a given story is to compare its assertions to any supporting evidence supplied, and to calibrate for vested interests and reliability as best we can. In cases where we are blessed with different accounts of the same event, we can do the evidence-to-assertion calculation for each of them and compare the results. Hardly a foolproof process, to be sure, but at least it engages the brain and gives reason a chance, unlike either blind trust or blind distrust.

That approach, however, would subject independent and corporate media to equal skepticism, require journalists to do journalism, and eliminate any default bias a narrative manager might wish to instill, which to a cynic could start to sound like an explanation for the *Washington Post*'s preference for the PropOrNot-style blacklist. A February 2021 *New York Times* article even openly advocated *against* critical thinking, arguing that it's better quickly to Google something to determine if a point of view is inside or outside the "consensus" than to get "bogged down" in evaluating evidence (Warzel 2021).

To be fair, it's not entirely bad advice to be careful about which rabbit holes you choose to go down – investigation is time-consuming and otherwise challenging – but obviously the inevitable result of trusting the received consensus as a general strategy will always be to reinforce rather than to challenge official narratives. It presumes that an official narrative cannot itself be disinformation, which, as incubator babies[6] and WMDs have robustly demonstrated, is a deeply unsound presumption.

Ironically enough, Walter Lippmann – along with Edward Bernays a key theoretician of propaganda – once expressed the hope that an improvement in the free press would come by the emergence of competition from "a great independent journalism, setting standards for commercial journalism," noting that "our sanity and, therefore, our safety depend upon this competition" (Lippmann 2010 [1920], p. 35,36). Now that this independent journalism has arrived, the disappointing response from the standard bearers has fallen somewhat short of the ideal predicted by Lippmann's capitalist theory.

The PropOrNot maneuver of invoking Russian disinformation was not an isolated instance, but reflected a broader effort that was, at least in part, driven by a secret policy. In 2018 and again in 2021, leaked documents exposed a covert network called the Integrity Initiative, in which academics and journalists, including Reuters and the BBC, were engaged in a military-intelligence-led anti-Russian propaganda effort funded by the British Foreign and Commonwealth Office (FCO). Reminiscent of the CIA's infamous Operation Mockingbird by virtue of its involvement of journalists in intelligence operations, the program also engaged in smearing left-wing and dissenting voices including Jeremy Corbyn (Elmaazi and Blumenthal 2018; McKeigue, Miller et al. 2018; Blumenthal 2021).

Contemporaneous with these efforts was the beginning of the push for Facebook, Google, Twitter, and other online platforms to take a more active role in filtering content for political reasons, beginning but not ending with alleged Russian disinformation. The social media giants did not initially seem eager to become the arbiters of truth, since their primary business interest is ostensibly in maximizing usage of their services, with little incentive to assume the liability or the costs of policing (Dwoskin, Dewey et al. 2016). The responsibility was first urged upon them by outsiders, but what began as a handful of journalists doing a bit of curating (ibid) soon became a partnership with the hawkish Atlantic Council – a think-tank and lobbying group that is part of the Atlantic Treaty Association, the goal of which is to "further the values" of NATO (Gabriel 2018).

Concern for NATO's opinion is now a core feature of social media content filtering. Twitter, for its part, in February 2021 announced (Twitter Safety 2021) it had deleted 373 accounts for unspecified links to Russia, Iran, and Armenia. The "Russia-linked" accounts were explicitly deleted because they were "undermining faith in the NATO alliance and its stability." The accounts with "ties" to Armenia were deleted because Twitter determined they wanted to "advance narratives…favorable to the Armenian government." The accounts that "appeared to originate in Iran" were deleted because they "were attempting to disrupt the public conversation during the first 2020 US Presidential Debate." Twitter's editorial head for Europe, the Middle East, and Africa is simultaneously a part-time British Army officer with the 77th Brigade, a psychological warfare unit dedicated to competing "in the war of narratives at the tactical level" (Cobain 2019).

However much these efforts characterize themselves as

fact-checking, it is impossible to ignore the overtly political elements of this social engineering exercise given the nature of the participants. Social media are not merely neutral platforms within which disinterested executives are just trying to make sure everyone gets their facts straight. They are the battlegrounds in the "war of narratives" that has explicitly been declared. Free and open discussion is not on the agenda.

The US Congress summoned social media CEOs to appear before them no fewer than three times between October 2020 and March 2021 for hearings on controlling online speech. What the hearings revealed was very much a broad and generalized approach to "hate speech, terrorist content, election disinformation and other harmful posts, photos and videos" to unspecified ends from unspecified sources who "had come to adopt Russia's playbook" (Romm, Lerman et al. 2020).

Banning speech about election fraud out of concern for the potential of inciting extremist violence is tricky territory indeed. It is, one must concede, within the bounds of the conceivable that disgruntled extremists, convinced of the government's irredeemable tyranny, might erupt into violent rebellion after being exposed to one too many inflammatory claims of electoral malfeasance against their preferred candidate. It is equally within the bounds of the conceivable, however, that such a volatile group might erupt into violent rebellion because of perceived infringements of any of their rights – such as speech rights – or, while we're at it, for any of a thousand other reasons.

More to the point, the freedom to criticize the government is the very heart of what the notion of free speech is all about. There is no constitutional or other legal stipulation that the criticism must be accurate, popular, or pleasant, or that it cannot invoke the possibility of fraud, corruption, or anything else. So narrative control measures about electoral fraud begin on extremely thin ice. The only way they could be made any worse would be if they were employed with broad imprecision.

In December of 2020 YouTube announced that it would begin removing any content that alleged "that widespread fraud or errors changed the outcome of the 2020 US Presidential election" (Taibbi 2020). This announcement came at a time when the sizable contingent of Trump voters who believed there had been election meddling were still stinging from the debacle of Twitter and Facebook temporarily blocking references to a pre-election *New York Post* story about evidence of corruption found on Hunter Biden's laptop (Greenwald 2020) – a story that was "denounced as Russian disinformation by virtually everyone in 'reputable' media" but which proved to be "a real story of legitimate public interest" (Taibbi 2020).

In any case, one of YouTube's first victims was a *Consortium News* "CN Live!" episode featuring journalist Greg Palast. Palast specializes in election shenanigans, having uncovered, for example, the Interstate Crosscheck program that illegally purged millions of mostly Democratic people of color from the voter registration rolls (Palast 2014). YouTube's ban of the CN Live! video came with the explanation that false claims about the presidential election were not allowed on the platform. But the removed episode had nothing to do with the presidential election and it made no false claims; it was about the January 5 Georgia election runoffs, and it documented Republican practices of "suppressing the vote...of black and other ethnic minority voters, who tend to vote Democratic" (Lauria 2021).

Consortium News appealed the YouTube decision. Despite the fact that the video had clearly not violated the questionable rule, the appeal was rejected. Whether this reflects algorithms run amok, bureaucratic inertia, bias against alternative media, or a generalized beyond-the-stated-rules attempt to suppress any information that "undermines faith" in elections, it certainly shows that justifications that nominally target the right can and will affect the left sooner or later (in this case sooner). It also shows that the principle of filtering content for political reasons deprives people of genuine, newsworthy journalism and has no place in a democracy. From a purely practical perspective, if your actual interest is in trying to reduce the threat represented by an already-agitated mass of possible extremists who are convinced they are being specifically targeted by a tyrannical conspiracy, banning or de-platforming the airing of their real or imagined grievances is also probably the most counterproductive step that it is possible to take.

This narrative control effort, with its unreason and its charges of Russian disinformation, is serious business, and nothing is immune to its lack of charm, not even science. Events in Syria provide an instructive example. Following the alleged chemical attack in Douma in Syria in April of 2018, the US, along with the UK and France, launched retaliatory missile strikes against the presumed culprit, the Assad government. The Organization for the Prohibition of Chemical Weapons (OPCW) began its investigation as the Western missiles were striking their targets. A long, involved, very interesting, and decidedly underreported series of events then took place. An important private dispute came to public light after the OPCW issued a final report asserting that there were "reasonable grounds [to conclude] that the use of a toxic chemical as a weapon took place" by way of two cylinders dropped from the sky, and that the chemical in question was "likely molecular chlorine" (OPCW 2019).

The problem? The findings were, according to one of the senior inspectors involved, a "complete turnaround [from] what the team had understood collectively during and after the Douma deployments" (Norton 2020). Thanks to a combination of leaked documents (OPCW Fact-Finding Mission 2019) and testimony from two senior inspectors – Ian Henderson and Gerald Whelan – (Hitchens 2020; Norton 2020), we now know that toxicology reports had found no evidence of chemical poisoning in the victims; that levels of chlorinated organic chemicals (COCs) at the scene were "no higher than you would expect in any household environment" (Steele 2019); and that the internal OPCW engineering assessment held that "the only plausible explanation for observations at the scene" was that both cylinders were "manually placed" at their respective locations, rather than dropped from aircraft (OPCW Fact-Finding Mission 2019). This evidence clearly indicated precisely the opposite of what the final report – produced without the involvement of the Douma investigative team – had concluded. The final report as issued implied that Assad had ordered a chemical attack; the team that actually investigated found evidence that implied that no such attack had occurred but that the scene had been staged by Al Nusra to look like one.

When the dissenting evidence was made public, things turned ugly. The evidence itself was ignored. Instead the inspectors were treated to an onslaught of ad hominem attacks and attempts to dismiss them as marginal figures and "disgruntled" employees (Higgins 2019). Fernando Arias, the OPCW Director-General, insisted: "[The inspectors] are not whistleblowers. They are individuals who could not accept that their views were not backed by evidence...their conclusions are erroneous, uninformed, and wrong" (OPCW 2020). US ambassador to the UN Kelly Clark characterized the inspectors' story as a "desperate and failed attempt by Russia to further spread disinformation"; Nicolas de Rivière, the French ambassador, also called it a "disinformation exercise"; Jonathan Allen, the UK ambassador, sneered at Henderson's "so-called evidence" (Mate 2020d). A *Guardian* article taking the OPCW claims at face value called the investigators' attempts to defend their team's work "a Russia-led campaign" (Wintour and McKernan 2020).

Obscured by the personal smears of the inspectors[7] was the more important question: where was the science that supposedly rendered their measurements and judgments irrelevant? Henderson noted that, apart from a vague assertion that three unidentified ballistics and engineering experts had done analyses that reversed the findings of the Douma team, there was "nothing new" in the final report to explain the reversal, "not even [an] attempt" to offer supporting facts (Henderson 2020). The inspectors asked for an open comparison of evidence in order to locate the source of the discrepancy – as scientists would routinely do in a normal world. The request was ignored.

Note that whether the inspectors were correct in their conclusions or not isn't the point. The point is that the normal processes of science were utterly disregarded in favor of an all-out, demonstrably dishonest narrative-control effort, in which mainstream journalism was an uncritical, witting participant.

There is a tabooing here that piques our surrealist interest. Foreign policy in general may not be a taboo subject for criticism, but when it comes to certain military and intelligence matters, there are clearly areas that seem not only to repel inquiry, but to nullify the thought of it, to rob it of legitimacy and respectability – to put the questioning outside of "normal" discourse or polite society.

As the Douma case demonstrates, even when the tellers of an inconvenient story are people who have spent long and dedicated careers toiling anonymously in the pursuit of science, building impeccable reputations; even when all they ask for is the observation of scientific norms of transparency; even when they are armed with as much data and expertise as anyone could ask for; and even when they're not the least bit Russian – against all that, the phrase "Russian disinformation" is still not only uttered and reported with a straight face but is, in stubborn defiance of reason, devastatingly effective. Just like that, evidence becomes "so-called evidence."

When transparent evidence is dismissed as so-called evidence while we're expected to accept hidden evidence as just plain evidence, something strange is going on. The normalization of this kind of behavior is better understood as a weirdification of reality. It signals that we ought to tread very carefully around claims of disinformation and other convenient shorthand methods of dismissing arguments without engaging them.

It evidently bears repeating that a democracy is, by design, an adversarial system that not only permits but requires – both in order to function and for its fundamental legitimacy – a thriving "marketplace of ideas." Open debate, free speech, a press that exercises its nominal freedom to challenge power, these are the sorts of things that pop up in any internet search for "lifeblood of democracy." The handful of examples of suppressed speech given here don't even scratch the surface of this unfortunate and apparently accelerating trend.

So, where are we after our whirlwind and arbitrary tour of potential Ur-fascist developments? We have a society whose symbolic order is constructed from notions of freedom, democracy, equality, and law, but whose actual characteristics include total surveillance, torture, indefinite detention, and arbitrary executive assassinations; the aggressive suppression of unwanted scientific information; the inappropriate use of anti-terror authority against dissenters and protesters; and concerted government-corporate efforts to silence, marginalize, discredit, or taboo certain kinds of political speech. Most of these features, if they are justified at all, are justified on national security grounds. Most of them, upon close scrutiny, see their justifications disintegrate and become potential ruptures in the symbolic order.

It is not important that we decide whether to apply the term fascism here. What is important is that a surrealist mode of inquiry is alert to repressive tendencies, and privileges the poking and prodding of these ruptures in order to stress test the dreamworld of the virtuous free democracy. It asks: Is this a society that welcomes dissent? Or is this a society that has marshaled its most powerful public and private resources to control it?

At issue within this anti-fascist element is not just what the state does to the people, but what the people are willing to accept as normal, the processes by which they do so, and the effects such normalization has on their lives. What a surrealist mode of inquiry brings to the task of contesting Ur-Fascism is a raising of the profile of the ways in which the machinery of repression is also a machinery of mystification, and the extent to which it implicates "that most terrible drug – ourselves – which we take in solitude" (Benjamin 1978, p. 54).

The mystified and repressed self is as good a segue as we're going to get into the next essential element of a surrealist mode of inquiry: Paranoia.

Chapter 3

Paranoia

[W]e are all, to varying degrees, paranoiacs; we are all occasionally haunted by the sense that we do not necessarily know the reality that we claim as the anchor of our subjectivity.
Jamer Hunt, Paranoia within Reason (1999, p. 29)

Just because you're paranoid doesn't mean they're not after you.
Usually attributed to Kurt Cobain or Joseph Heller

Paranoia, as a concomitant of narrative skepticism and gravitating toward the tabooed, is essential to the logic of a surrealist mode of inquiry. Indeed in an age dominated by total surveillance, terrorism, counterterrorism, fake news, and conspiracy theories, the paranoid element of surrealism has never been more relevant. "Paranoid art is the ultimate opposite, the urgent opposite, of complacent art" (Lethem 2012).

The surrealist interest in paranoia is, like the surrealist interest in crime, a function of what Jonathan Eburne (2008) calls the movement's noir period of the 1930s. Since this noir period was, for the original surrealists, a time of political recalibration following their brief and disappointing entry into normal anti-fascist politics, a discussion of paranoia with reference to surrealpolitik follows naturally from the previous chapter.

In the case of the original surrealists' anti-fascism, much has been written about their ill-fated alliance with the French communist party, and the effects on the surrealist movement of association with what they soon recognized as Stalinism. The political experience of surrealism in this regard was described by Jean Paul Sartre as "a pathetic failure" (Beaujour 1963, p. 90). Referring to Breton and his cohorts, Raoul Vaneigem has written that "these young people, who ought by rights to have turned themselves into theorists and practitioners of the revolution of everyday life, were content to be mere artists thereof, waging a war of mere harassment against bourgeois society as though it fell to the Communist Party alone to mount the main offensive" (1999 [1977], p. 39).

In the wake of this unsatisfactory experience, an evolution in surrealist thinking occurred, and a different kind of political engagement emerged that remained truer to surrealist artistic principles while extending the movement into new and somewhat darker territory marked by a fascination with paranoia and spectacular crime. The theoretical move made by surrealism toward paranoia was as much a logical forward progression for the movement as a reaction to failure, since surrealism began in the first instance "by appropriating all the advantages of madness" (Rosemont 1989b) at its inception. It is this broadening of scope that enables a surrealist angle on anti-fascism to highlight the notion of a linkage between consensus reality-narratives and the mechanisms of delusion. This is the heart of surrealpolitik.

Both an aesthetic and an ethical concern, as Adorno observed, "the tension in Surrealism that is discharged in shock is the tension between schizophrenia and reification" (Adorno 1991 [1956], p. 88). In a reified reality narrative, subjects become objects – passive, fixed, fated – and objects become subjects – active determinants of an inevitable order. Social and economic relationships, for example, become a "natural" function of "the way things are" rather than the result of choices and power relationships. Radical change becomes unimaginable. Everything is too orderly, too organized, too real to be re-imagined. "It is what it is." Schizophrenia, on the other hand, is marked by utterly disorganized thought, with nothing stable, nothing fixed, a great difficulty in separating the real from the unreal. If reification reflects an excess of realism, schizophrenia reflects a dearth. What Adorno has appreciated about surrealism is the power of the latter to disrupt the former, to expose its pretensions, which is to do the work called for by Fisher, i.e., to take the real out of capitalist realism. Hence the tension, which creates in its release the shock of the reified suddenly rendered contingent and fluid, with assumptions about reality upended and in disarray.

The relationship between delusion and reification can also be described in terms of Lacan's big Other. The discrepancy between what is actually known and what the big Other is allowed to know is a source of both tension and release for a society, enabling it to function but containing the seeds of its potential undoing. There is both an illicit pleasure and a sense of agency in the private act of differentiating oneself from the stories insisted upon by the big Other, without which those stories would quickly become less tolerable. Thus the discrepancy permits the persistence of collective fictions, but it also creates potentially disruptive oppositional conditions. "In spite of all its grounding power, the big Other…exists only in so far as subjects *act as if it exists*" (Žižek 2006, Kindle location 185, emphasis in the original). The possibility of undermining capitalist realism's realism relies on nurturing this process of undermining the big Other's givens and transgressing its taboos to the point where differentiation reaches the hoped-for critical mass.

The big Other's narratives include fictions intended to sustain a social mythology along the lines, for example, of American Exceptionalism (Duquette 2013) or capitalist realism. The extent to which the big Other represents a fundamental deception is an open question. Certainly Fisher's argument is predicated on the expectation that the deception is fundamental, far-reaching, and insufficiently questioned. This possibility suggests the notion that society – particularly perhaps American society – might be suffering from what one might call "cultural gaslighting."

Gaslighting became a psychological term of art in therapy in the 1980s and is now regularly used (and abused) colloquially (Abramson 2014). Deriving from the 1944 film *Gaslight* (and/or the play and earlier film that preceded it), the term denotes the imposition of a false reality, "a form of emotional manipulation in which the gaslighter tries (consciously or not) to induce in someone the sense that her reactions, perceptions, memories and/or beliefs are not just mistaken, but utterly without grounds—paradigmatically, so unfounded as to qualify as crazy" (Abramson 2014, p. 2).

Extending this concept of gaslighting to a cultural level goes beyond the usual jaded recognition of corruption, e.g., the expectation of a certain amount of lying and greed among our politicians. Cultural gaslighting implies a more total hoodwinking at the level of capitalist realism or a national security ontology, an imposition of a whole set of ersatz socio-political assumptions. Examples might include the constant invocation of false threats (Ponsonby 2005 [1928]), significant instances of which have been exposed: the Soviet missile gap never existed (Licklider 1970); the Gulf of Tonkin incident did not happen (Moïse 1996); Iraq had no weapons of mass destruction (Ritter 2005). The question becomes: Are these events merely anomalies within a generally trustworthy narrative, or are they ruptures that reveal a hidden, fundamentally different reality? Or are such questions "utterly without grounds" – is it crazy to ask?

Say: This is real, the world is real, the real exists (I have met it) – no one laughs. Say: This is a simulacrum, you are merely a simulacrum, this war is a simulacrum – everyone bursts out laughing. With forced, condescending laughter, or uncontrollable mirth, as though at a childish joke or an obscene proposition. Everything to do with the simulacrum is taboo or obscene, as is everything related to sex or death. Yet it is much rather reality and obviousness which are obscene. It is the truth we should laugh at. You can imagine a culture where everyone laughs spontaneously when someone says: "This is true", "This is real". (Baudrillard 2008)

Despite the checkered history of official claims preceding and during wartime, skepticism among mainstream journalists has not become notably more prevalent (see for example Carden 2017). When assertions of dire new threats are made, to use Baudrillard's phrase, "no one laughs." A surrealist mode of inquiry problematizes this lack of laughter. Its effort here to multiply uncertainty is, in this light, ultimately not so much an attack on facts and rationality as a search for them.

Surrealism's interest in paranoia is nowhere better represented than in Salvador Dali's development of his paranoiac-critique, as articulated for example in his 1930 essay "The Rotting Donkey," originally published in *Le Surréalisme au service de la revolution* (Dali 2004 [1930]), and in the writings of René Crevel and Jacques Lacan in the surrealist journal *Minotaure*.

Dali's argument recognizes "the image of desire hidden behind the simulacra of terror"; paranoia here represents a thought process that promises the ability "to systematize confusion and thereby contribute to a total discrediting of the world of reality" (Dali 2004 [1930], p. 257). This, for a surrealist, is a good thing, presuming as it does that the reality in question deserves to be discredited. Dali speaks of reality as comprising multiplicities of images, simulacra competing to attain "the highest potential for existence." The effect of considering that one's reality is one among a host of competing images is to break down certainties by destroying ideologically derived confidence in any given alternative. Dali's method "reasserts an often lost continuity between the delusional and rational – retying the knot of their mutual genesis" (Hunt 1999, p. 21).

Paranoia became "a means for the modernist withdrawal from consensual language...[forming] a bridge between the unconscious of the individual and the mass" (Constantinidou 2010, p. 131-132). This is where surrealist paranoia calls back to the element of dreamwork, as discussed previously – our periodic reminder that all the elements I have separated into different chapters are mutually reinforcing and indeed become a seamless whole in a surrealist mode of inquiry.

Proceeding from Lacan's then-recent doctoral thesis, René Crevel in his "Notes Towards a Psycho-dialectic" (2004 [1933]) similarly describes the "paranoiac psychosis" not as a purely mental dysfunction but as an interactivity between subjective experience and objective external reality, so that understanding it becomes a matter of "throwing light upon the inside as well as the outside" (p. 266). The surrealist view of paranoia was that it was like a "highly sensitive microscope" through which "we notice the interdependence of internal and external phenomena" (ibid.). What Lacan called paranoia's "new syntax" was taken by the surrealists as "a representation of complex structures of social and psychological determination that could be mobilized for the sake of political understanding" (Eburne 2008, p. 180).

The arguments of Dali and Crevel echo the idea of interrogating the assumptions of the Lacanian big Other from the inside out, in other words as a critique of what we've internalized rather than of some purely external construction. The feedback loop that is constituted by learned beliefs and confirmation bias is, at the same time, the fundamental mechanism of both delusion and ordinary socialization. To question the symbolic order is to question your own mind. Looking for cracks in the foundation of your own internal construction of reality can be a terrifying prospect in any case, and is made more so when the limb you go out on takes you beyond the comforts of society's consensual normal. There is no avoiding an encounter with madness in a surrealist mode of inquiry. In any attempt to take the real out

54

of realism, whether capitalist realism, national security realism, or any other kind, one finds oneself face to face with questions of delusion. Disillusionment normally has connotations of bitterness and disappointment, yet the shedding of unhealthy illusions is a powerful form of liberation. Before they can be shed, they have to be identified, and that process requires a mind that is not only critical but courageous.

The determination of labels like insane or paranoid, not unlike the determination of what constitutes terrorism or security or freedom, is substantially a question of power relationships – which is not to say that these concepts never correspond to realities or that determinations can never be made, but that there is a good case to be made for treading very carefully. As psychologist David Rosenhan put it in his study of whether medical professionals could tell the sane from the insane in a clinical setting, "Whenever the ratio of what is known to what needs to be known approaches zero, we tend to invent 'knowledge' and assume that we understand more than we actually do" (Rosenhan 1973, p. 257).

Our previous acknowledgment of the porousness of the borders between our dreaming and waking lives suggests analogous uncertainties between the sane and the insane. Whether we lose our confidence in reality completely or cling to our illusions too tightly, sanity itself becomes contested territory. Sanity, like reality, is fungible and subject to internal and external interpretations.

"From the moment I entered the insane ward on the Island," wrote Nellie Bly of infiltrating an asylum for journalistic purposes, "I made no attempt to keep up the assumed *role* of insanity. I talked and acted just as I do in ordinary life. Yet strange to say, the more sanely I talked and acted the crazier I was thought to be." (Bly 2011 [1887], p. 7) By nearly a century later, that problem had not been solved. In the early 1970s, Rosenhan conducted an experiment by getting sane "pseudopatients" admitted to psychiatric hospitals. He found that "[h]owever much we may be personally convinced that we can tell the normal from the abnormal, the evidence is simply not compelling...the normal are not detectably sane" (Rosenhan 1973, p. 250). As the original surrealists themselves put it in 1925 in an open "Letter to the Head Doctors of Insane Asylums": "Laws and customs have given you the right to examine the mind. Your understanding enables you to exercise this sovereign jurisdiction. What a laugh!" (Richardson and Fijalkowski 2001, p. 140)

The misdiagnosis of justified true beliefs as crazy is a well-recognized phenomenon. It even has a name: the Martha Mitchell Effect, after the wife of John Mitchell, the US Attorney General in the early 1970s (Colman 2009). Martha made accusations of illegal activities going on in the White House that were deemed so off the wall that they were dismissed as the delusions of a mentally ill woman. She was eventually vindicated by the famous revelations that brought down a presidency, earning her the nickname "the Cassandra of Watergate" (Wikipedia).

The Cassandra reference is of additional interest to surrealists. In Greek mythology Cassandra was given the power of prophecy by Apollo, but when she rejected his advances he also gave her the curse that nobody would believe her warnings. In Nietzschean (2000 [1872]) terms, the Apollonian is the rational and orderly half of a dualistic tension with Dionysian ecstatic revelry. A surrealist approach to questions of sanity and delusion (and everything else) of course takes the Dionysian position against an Apollonian rationality that, as in the Cassandra myth, may be employed to deceitful ends.

In her memoir *Down Below* (2017 [1944]), Leonora Carrington was in part "redirecting paranoiac theory toward contemporary surrealist thinking about collective social myths" (Eburne 2008, p. 218). As she processed her own flight from fascism and the arrest of her lover, Max Ernst, by the Gestapo, she became "convinced that parts of Europe were becoming hypnotized by agents of Hitler" (Hertz 2010, p. 100). From her own later vantage point in *Down Below*, she demonstrates that analyzing paranoia can reveal as much about society and health as it does about illness by examining subjectivity from the perspective of social signifiers. Carrington understood the political use-value of paranoia as deriving from its characterization of "accepted formulas" – ideological forces – as a "thick layer of filth" that must be purged, first of all from herself, and also from society, in order for there to be a liberation of the surreal kind – a liberation of the imagination.

There is another side to this coin. If one risk is that insidious fictions have distorted the political imaginary and marginalized justified true beliefs into the realm of the seemingly improbable, the opposite risk is sliding down a slippery slope of genuine paranoid delusion. Once it is appreciated that the symbolic order is maintained, at times and in part, by liars, gaslighters, and propagandists, it can become very easy to believe anything as long as it is not an officially sanctioned narrative. "Don't believe anything until it's been officially denied" is a useful enough rule of thumb – until officials deny something that's actually false. Like the gap between what people can know and what the big Other can know, the territory between sober skepticism and spurious fantasy is creative ground that is ripe for surrealist provocation. Yet the questions rightly put when paranoid delusion is suspected – questions of evidence – are the very same questions that a surrealist mode of inquiry puts to the big Other.

While liberating oneself from consensual reality may be as likely to lead to a crippling derangement as to any form of enlightenment, it is a necessary risk if one is to free oneself from illusion and resist, for example, the effects of skillful propaganda. It is those questions of evidence, and the separation of evidence from "so-called evidence," that are essential to navigating these waters without drowning.

This abstract, theoretical interest in paranoia can be applied in various more tangible ways to our subject, the national security state. The issue has particular resonance, for example, with reference to the relationship between intelligence agencies and terrorist groups, which can appear to be a maddening "hall of mirrors" in which we variously train, establish, welcome, infiltrate, and support our nominal enemies by calculations that are either ruthlessly cynical or have gone very much awry, or both (see for example Sanger 2012; Mekhennet 2014; Ahmed 2015; Cartalucci 2015; Fisk 2015; Milne 2015; Norton-Taylor 2015; Porter 2016). As a fount of numerous potential unrealities, the terrorism-intelligence nexus invites the artistic paranoia that a ceaselessly questioning surrealist mode is so ready to provide. A take-nothing-for-granted questioning of reality confronts terrorism and counterterrorism in the center of that hall of mirrors, one paranoia reflecting another.

On one side of the mirror are the much-maligned conspiracy theories, commonly considered to be pathologically paranoid. Because the term "conspiracy theory" is almost always used as a pejorative (Featherstone 2000; Sunstein and Vermeule 2008; Heilbrunn 2011; Kay 2011; Mortimer 2015; Oaklander 2015), one could be forgiven the impression that political paranoia is the exclusive purview of obsessive, delusional fantasists, even if some of them are otherwise "more or less normal people" (Hofstadter 1964, p. 77).

This impression, however, is demonstrably and profoundly false. The other side of the mirror is an utterly normalized mainstream political environment that is quite obviously brimming with paranoid conspiracy theories from stem to stern. Paranoia and plots are so thoroughly the water in which we swim that we do not always recognize them by those names.

Theories about conspiracies are everywhere; the United States was literally founded on them. The men who drafted the Federalist Papers and the US Constitution presumed that representative democracy was vulnerable to – in their own words – "conspiracies against the people's liberties" by "perfidious public officials" and to "tyrannical designs" by "oppressive factions" (deHaven-Smith 2013, p. 55). The United States is a nation that has long considered itself besieged, from the Cold War threat of reds under beds to today's New York City subway slogan "if you see something, say something." If it's not Russia meddling in our elections or sowing disinformation, it's terrorists, and increasingly domestic terrorists, lurking in every dissenting shadow. Conspiracy theories are intrinsically neither remarkable nor ridiculous. They are simply theories that posit something that happens all the time: two or more people agreeing to commit a crime. The theories are as ubiquitous as the conspiracies; hundreds of them are alleged and proven every year in US courtrooms under the Racketeer Influenced and Corrupt Organization (RICO) Act.

What is intriguing then is the question of why the term conspiracy theory retains any tabooing power at all, let alone with the effectiveness it clearly has in marginalizing a line of inquiry. If it were simply a matter of evidence, with poorly supported theories going into the nut-job bin and well-supported ones into the public record of historical reality, the situation would be very much more comforting but very much less interesting. But this is not at all the case. We have already seen in the previous chapter how little evidence matters in establishing a reality narrative, and we shall see several more examples in the pages ahead. Indeed the fascination for a surrealist approach begins with the observation that – despite so many examples of "facts being fixed" (Van Natta Jr. 2006) around narratives, as in the Iraq War, and unwelcome evidence being ignored or dismissed, as in several cases in Syria (Carden 2017) – the suggestion, for example, that a given justification for war might be a mere pretext is still normally treated with that special derision reserved for the most unhinged of drooling moon-howlers.

The complications don't stop with evidence-free narratives and contrary evidence being ignored. The very fact of having assembled evidence can be seen as evidence of insanity. As Richard Hofstadter has noted, "respectable paranoid literature carefully and all but obsessively accumulates 'evidence'" not, in Hofstadter's view, to convince a "hostile world" so much as "to protect [the paranoid's] cherished convictions from it" (Hofstadter 1964, p. 85). The implication of the scare quotes around "evidence" of course is that evidence produced by a paranoid person is bound to be dubious: the "so-called evidence" we encountered in the anti-fascism chapter. Hofstadter acknowledges that "the idea of the paranoid style as a force in politics would have little contemporary relevance or historical value if it were applied only to men with profoundly disturbed minds" and that what makes it significant is its use by "more or less normal people"; he further acknowledges that the paranoid style "has more to do with the way in which ideas are believed and advocated than with the truth or falsity of their content."

What is interesting then about Hofstadter's perfectly accurate observation is that, true or not, crazy or not, evidence in a paranoid style comes with implicit scare quotes, and the more evidence that is presented, the worse it gets. When a strident votary pins a non-initiate down with an overwhelming amount of detailed evidence of a conspiracy regarding, for example, the fate of John F. Kennedy or World Trade Center Building 7, what is immediately obvious to the person on the receiving end is something that has nothing to do with assassinations or controlled demolitions: that the proselytizer has spent an unconventional quantity of time on the subject, is in the fever grip of an obsession, has crossed the bridge out of normal town. In short, the very profusion of evidence makes the person seem crazed. It is a question, as Hofstadter notes, of style. It is a rare person whose fashion sense will recommend joining the journey over that bridge.

The recipient is likely to have the simultaneous awareness that the assertions are in principle falsifiable/verifiable, on the one hand, and on the other that falsification/verification would require time and energy that is simply not going to be made available. Just the awareness of the probable existence of counter-arguments, even without knowing what they might be, may be enough to produce the wary and amused facial expression that the proselytizer has grown so accustomed to seeing, making the look in his eye even wilder, his tone even more exasperated. Furthermore, even if the argument has fully convinced its target intellectually, the aesthetic of the thing – *the style* – may prevent its adoption and elicit the same facial expression regardless. Thus, even when the devoted conspiracist wins the intellectual battle, he may only succeed in digging himself into a deeper hole with every shovelful of evidence he places on the pile.

All of this is grist for the surrealist mill, which already recognizes the complex and arbitrary mirroring nature of the reality-delusion relationship. There is an anti-paranoid style, too, in politics. Hofstadter's formulation can, after all, be reversed: the dismissal of the paranoid "evidence" might be less a concern for what is true and more a way of protecting the non-paranoid's "cherished convictions" from it. None of the foregoing should be taken to imply that there is a sharp, clear division between paranoia and normal town. That bridge sees a lot of traffic, and many of those who don't cross it spend time on it gazing at the river flowing beneath.

One of the ways of describing the difference between the two types of conspiracy theories – the ones that are widely held up as objects of scorn and the ones we consume unperturbed in the news with our morning coffee – is in terms of compatibility or lack thereof with the beliefs of the big Other. A tension arises from our efforts variously to conform to and distinguish ourselves from that symbolic order, e.g., to be socially acceptable while protecting our more idiosyncratic personal views. It is that space between the official narratives and the thoughts we entertain in private or on the margins that provides such fertile soil for a surrealist mode of inquiry.

As an example of the gap between sanctioned and unsanctioned thought, it remains taboo even after more than half a century for a major newspaper to take the idea of a JFK assassination conspiracy seriously, even though that is precisely what a majority of US citizens have long believed (Swift 2013). The same kind of taboo is even stronger regarding the more recent events of September 11, 2001, yet over a third of US citizens – and half of New Yorkers – believe that elements of the US government either "assisted in the 9/11 attacks" or had foreknowledge of the attacks and "consciously failed to act" (Zogby International 2004; Hargrove 2006).

The prevalence of these conspiratorial views says nothing about their relationship to the truth – similar percentages of US citizens also believe in creationism (Swift 2017) and angels (Associated Press 2011). It says a good deal, however, about the relationship between the privately held views of individuals and the big Other. It suggests that behind the decorum of our implicit agreements regarding a consensual normal lies a tension between rational and irrational, paranoia and practicality, fact and fiction. This is one basis of the tension that a surrealist mode of inquiry seeks to exploit in its investigations. That tension from "the madness that one locks up" (Breton 2010 [1924], p. 5), however, is also heightened by the troubled empirical grounds upon which conspiracy theories are either mainstreamed or marginalized.

The existence of widespread yet illicit and often invisible private beliefs indicate a contested psycho-political space that confirms paranoia's importance as a signature element of a surrealist mode of inquiry. This mode of inquiry is informed by documented ruptures in the historical terrorism narrative, which lend the surrealist approach a certain currency by underscoring that these blurry or dreamlike realities are not merely an intellectual conceit. Notable examples of major ruptures of this kind include the exposures of Operation Northwoods and Operation Gladio.

Operation Gladio was a NATO program, begun in the immediate aftermath of World War II, the purpose of which was to establish secret paramilitary organizations – "stay behind armies" – in multiple European countries nominally to fight behind enemy lines in the event of a Soviet invasion (Ganser 2004). These well-armed paramilitaries predominantly comprised Nazi or neo-Nazi far-right members, and reported directly to intelligence agencies rather than through regular military channels. Their existence was in many cases entirely unknown to their host countries' leaders.

As a result of an Italian investigation led by judge Felice Casson, it was established that several terrorist attacks that had long been blamed on leftist groups were actually the work of Gladio cells. Judge Casson explained that Gladio was a "strategy of tension," the purpose of which was "to promote conservative, reactionary social and political tendencies" (Ganser 2004, p. 7). Gladio was successfully kept secret for more than 40 years before its eventual exposure. The furor from the Italian case led to Gladio's exposure in other European countries, including the United Kingdom. "As the Gladio scandal erupted in 1990 the British press observed that 'it is now clear that the elite Special Air Service regiment (SAS) was up to its neck in the NATO scheme, and functioned, with MI6, as a training arm for guerrilla warfare and sabotage'." (Ganser 2004, p. 44. Internal quote from *Searchlight*, January 1991.)

Operation Northwoods, made public in 1997 as part of a document declassification mandated by the Assassination Records Review Board, proposed the performance of terror attacks within the United States, to be blamed on Cuba as a way to justify overt military action against Castro. That plan was rejected by President Kennedy only after being authorized by the US Joint Chiefs of Staff (Davis 2006). One can argue that its rejection proves that such deceptive "false flag" attacks – attacks carried out by one party in such a way as to be blamed on another – are unlikely to be perpetrated by the United States, or conversely that it was only thwarted in this instance by an extraordinary president. In either case, it provides a disturbing glimpse into the mindset of the defense-intelligence establishment, at least at one point in time. It proves, if nothing else, that false flag attacks orchestrated by the United States are far from unthinkable: they've definitely been thought about. There can be no argument about that.

The historical record therefore shows unequivocally that terrorist attacks are not always what they seem, and that, despite the intuitively reasonable objections that "it would involve too many people" or "somebody would talk," massive conspiracies can indeed be kept secret for long periods of time. The paranoia-inviting questions raised include: How far might this sort of thing go? Has the full extent of it already been revealed? Given the uncontested facts that we do know, on what rational basis ought we to be sanguine in our contempt of (unsanctioned) conspiracy theories? These questions hark back to the specter of cultural gaslighting as previously described. Paranoia in a surrealist mode of inquiry is indispensable to negotiating this slippery, post-9/11, post-truth netherworld and the mechanisms by which narratives become or fail to become accepted as facts.

Attempts to shift the terrorism/security discourse via realism – citing facts, as above – is an appeal to the rational. Apart from the observation that this is not the surrealist way – the "realistic attitude…feeds on and derives strength from the newspapers and stultifies both science and art by assiduously flattering the lowest of tastes; clarity bordering on stupidity, a dog's life" (Breton 2010 [1924], p. 6) – it is no easy task to change political opinions with facts (Lindström 1997). Facts, while indispensable, are often received warily, quite rightly, as they always require verification, context, and interpretation. Still, the problem of determining what is actually going on and what it means is acute at the present historical moment, when accusations of "fake news" are glibly exchanged as a way of walling off competing and irreconcilable narratives that often reject and ignore rather than engage and debate each other.

It is for such reasons that paranoia in a surrealist mode does not rely on pushing contestable facts and unresolvable arguments, but favors seducing the imagination and eroding the foundations of our unconscious assumptions. A surrealist mode of inquiry is not necessarily superior to an "ordinary" realist approach, but it is a useful complement. There is a futile circularity to the proposition of throwing more facts at a mindset known precisely for its resistance to empirical evidence. Facts and rationality are clearly necessary tools for accessing truth but just as clearly insufficient. Terrorism discourse has suffered from what Michael Taussig has called "the politics of epistemic murk and the fiction of the real" (1987, p. xiii) to the point where debate quickly encounters taboo. The situation suggests the need for alternative approaches. "If mere words, the language of public discourse, are debased, the writer may well wish to turn to more intuitive models of communication, the discourse of private symbolism and even madness" (Scanlan 2001, p. 81).

In highlighting the role of power and ideology in establishing political narratives that have illusory aspects, a paranoid surrealist mode seeks "to penetrate the veil while retaining its hallucinatory quality" (Taussig 1984, p. 472):

The political and artistic problem is to engage with that, to maintain that hallucinatory quality while effectively turning it against itself. That would be the true catharsis, the great counterdiscourse whose poetics we must ponder in the political terrain now urgently exposed today. (Taussig 1984, p. 472)

The idea is to use paranoia as a tool to make uncomfortable questions unavoidable, to inspire both the act of questioning and a tolerance for the unresolved, and to entertain "the possibility of a real, built by the rational, anchored by the delusional" (Hunt 1999).

Such considerations substantially comprise the rationale for a surrealist mode of inquiry's disorienting strategy – an alternative "strategy of tension" conceived as a sort of aesthetic-psychological counterpoint to the one employed by Operation Gladio. We know enough to wonder more about why we think we know what we think we know.

Chapter 4

Spectacular Crime

The simplest Surrealist act consists of dashing down into the street, pistol in hand, and firing blindly, as fast as you can pull the trigger, into the crowd.

André Breton, Second Manifesto of Surrealism (2010 [1930], p. 125)

This is the story of a crime – of the murder of reality. And the extermination of an illusion – the vital illusion, the radical illusion of the world. The real does not disappear into illusion; it is illusion that disappears into integral reality.

Jean Baudrillard, The Perfect Crime (2008, p. xi)

Crime is one of the less obvious signature elements of surrealism, yet the surrealist movement clearly had a sustained fascination with the subject, particularly spectacular crime, the sort – like terrorism – that dominates front pages. From Breton's "simplest Surrealist act" to Jean Clair explicitly blaming the September 11 attacks on "the Surrealist ideology" (Clair 2001), surrealism's linkage with the crime of terrorism is clear, albeit complex. I'm particularly indebted here to Jonathan Eburne's seminal *Surrealism and the Art of Crime* (2008), which makes the definitive case for the depth of the surrealist engagement with spectacular violence.

Surrealism's political evolution away from party politics to its "noir" period was marked by a shift in its primary journals, from the Marxist heavy-handedness of *La Surréalisme au Service de la Révolution* to the more artistically innovative *Minotaure*, which reflected a revived interest in the unconscious and deviancy, as well as crime and terror. In this period:

[Surrealism's] mannered proliferation of stylistic motifs exceeds its own formalism in order to evoke latent forces of terror and social dissolution at work in "reality"...Its political use-value lies in its reassessment of the moral and epistemological bases of Surrealism's political platform, in response to a historical moment rapidly becoming – to cite the title of an article in *Minotaure 3-4* – an "Age of Fear". (Eburne 2003, p. 94)

We, too, live in an age of fear, and the political use-value made of crime by surrealism in the 1930s is similarly important to a surrealist examination of the national security state today. If not for the fear of terrorism, the various indignities now associated with going through an airport, to say nothing of the loss of so many civil liberties, would not be tolerated. Fear itself is ripe for exploration in a surrealist mode, subject as it is to considerable irrationality, and nowhere more so than in the realm of "terrorist phantasmagoria" (Douglass and Zulaika 1996, introduction, p. x).

Terrorism discourse is characterized by the confusion of sign and context provoked by the deadly atrocity of apparently random acts, the impossibility of discriminating reality from make-believe, and text from reader. These strange processes and their mix make terrorism a queer phenomenon...[N]othing appears to be more damaging to the ghosts and myths of terrorism...than fictionalizing them further to the point that fear dissolves into "as-if" terror. The discourse's victory, then, derives from imposing a literal frame of "this *is* real war," "this *is* global threat," "this *is* total terror." Its defeat derives from writing "this is an *as-if* war," "this is an *as-if* global threat," "this is *make-believe* total terror." (Douglass and Zulaika 1996, p. 28-29.)

The confusion of sign and context into a Baudrillard-esque hyperreality is exacerbated by the complex relationship between media and war. Freedman and Thussu have noted that the Iraq War was "more than a catalogue of errors" but was "shaped for coverage, planned and formatted, pre-produced and aired with high production values, designed to persuade, not just inform," describing this state of affairs as a "crime against democracy" (Freedman and Thussu 2012, p. 314-315). Systematic attempts to undermine the nominal functions of the political system represent "another category of offenses, described by the French poet André Chenier as '*les crimes puissants qui font trembler les lois*,' crimes so great that they make the laws themselves tremble" and from which "we recoil in a general failure of imagination and nerve" (Sick 1991, p. 226). I propose that these kinds of crimes lend themselves well to consideration in a surrealist mode since they may betray our fundamental notions of the rules of reality.

Surrealism's interest in spectacular crime, both real and fictional, dates to its earliest activities, e.g., its fascination with the Fantômas crime serials, "whose basic premise was the master villain's capacity for entering and escaping locked rooms and impossible situations" (Eburne 2008, p. 38). Indeed a keen interest in crime was fundamental to the development of surrealism, and is indispensable to the task of bringing a surrealist mode of inquiry to bear on the national security state.

There are many examples of the surrealist fascination with crime, of which I will name but a few just to establish the motif. The surrealists were deeply obsessed with the Comte de Lautréamont and the Marquis de Sade from the beginning of the movement. The former was the originator of the phrase "as beautiful as the chance encounter of a sewing machine and an umbrella on a dissecting table," perhaps the primary inspiration for the surrealist style of language play. He also wrote *Les Chants de Maldoror*, which, as with the works of

Sade, frequently depicted scenes of torture, murder, and rape. These scenes were defended as provocative critiques of moral and social laws by such surrealists as Paul Éluard and André Masson, whose *Massacres* series celebrating "the dionysiac spirit" was produced as a reaction against surrealism's political engagement with communism (Monahan 2001, p. 708).

"Au Clair de la lune" by Philippe Soupault (writing as Philippe Weil), a kind of locked-room mystery, appeared in the May 1922 issue of the Dadaist/surrealist journal *Littérature*. An emotionless and detailed crime scene inventory, removed from any broader frame of reference, Soupault's narrative, rather than eliminating impossibilities and uncertainties to arrive at a narrow and definite resolution, as in a traditional police procedural or detective story, "instead multiplies this doubt through its very surfeit of evidence" (Eburne 2008, p. 28). The multiplication of doubt and of possibilities is essential both to original surrealist thought and to the strategy of applying a surrealist mode of inquiry to the national security state. The paradoxical confounding effect of a "surfeit" of evidence also recalls the paranoid style as described in the previous chapter.

The surrealists also shone their spotlight, if not in celebration then certainly without opprobrium, on a few murderers, particularly young female ones, notably Germaine Berton, a 20-year-old anarchist who assassinated a prominent right-wing royalist; 18-year-old Violette Nozière, who murdered her father to put an end to years of sexual abuse; a woman known only as Aimée, who stabbed an actress and tried to strangle a publisher; and the Papin sisters Christine and Léa, cook and housekeeper in a *haute bourgeois* household, who bludgeoned their employers to death with a hammer and pulled their eyes out with their bare hands. The Papin sisters were also the subject of "Motives of Paranoiac Crime," the first published essay by Jacques Lacan, in the surrealist journal *Minotaure* (Lacan 1933). This fascination was justified on the grounds that "[t]he beauty of certain assaults upon modesty, or upon life, is that they accuse, with all their violence, the monstrosity of laws and the constraints that make monsters." (Crevel 2004 [1933], p. 266)

The surrealist interest in spectacular crime and what it revealed about social mores, patriarchy, repression, and so on – in short crime-and-society as a device through which to privilege surrealism's political and ethical concerns – extends too into the realm of fiction, and not least of all pulp detective fiction. Surrealists Léo Malet and Boris Vian both experimented with the form of the detective novel, the latter writing, for example, the extremely absurd *To Hell with the Ugly*, accurately described by its translator as "like a pornographic Hardy Boys novel set on the Island of Dr Moreau to a be-bop soundtrack" (Vian 2011 [1948]).

Gilles Deleuze, writing in celebration of the *Série Noire* crime fiction series founded by surrealist pioneer Marcel Duhamel, noted that these were no ordinary detective novels. Detective work here "has nothing to do with a metaphysical or scientific search for truth" but rather a multiplication of unscrupulous but compensated errors revealing "the power of the false" that "permits a society, at the limits of cynicism, to hide that which it wishes to hide, to show that which it wishes to show, to deny evidence and proclaim the implausible" (Deleuze 2001).

The use of literature to highlight deception and the fragility of purported reality with specific reference to terrorism is far from new, and is certainly appropriate in a discussion that is, after all, about the intermingling of fact and fiction. By the very beginning of the twentieth century, Joseph Conrad's *The Secret Agent* (2015 [1907]) was already immersed in misdirection, false flags, and the various difficulties of determining responsibility when bombs explode at random. While the novel predates surrealism and is not particularly dreamlike, it remains notable in this context for the terrorism currency in which it does trade: uncertainty and mystification. It is so redolent of themes associated with modern conspiracy theories that it's worth a brief recap.

Set in the London of 1886, *The Secret Agent* tells the story of a bombing attributed to an ineffective group of anarchists, but actually done at the bidding of a foreign power desirous of seeing a more repressive Britain. Conrad's protagonist, Mr Verloc, a member of the anarchist group who doubles as an agent of the unnamed foreign country's embassy, is called by that embassy's First Secretary, a Mr Vladimir, to receive his instructions:

"England must be brought into line...What they want just now is a jolly good scare...A series of outrages...executed here in this country; not only *planned* here – that would not do – they would not mind. Your friends could set half the Continent on fire without influencing the public opinion here in favour of a universal repressive legislation." (Conrad 2015 [1907], p. 20-21)

What we have in *The Secret Agent* is not a repressive state pushing back against terrorism, but falsified terrorism providing the pretext for an increase in repression – not unlike the "strategy of tension" we saw with Operation Gladio in the previous chapter, suggesting that the tactic is more time-honored than wildly implausible. The repression is in itself a desired end, a mechanism of control of the fear-based society. The attack in the novel is literally and figuratively an assault on reason: the bomb was intended to explode in the Greenwich Observatory (but explodes prematurely by accident) – an attack on science. "The attack must have all the shocking senselessness of gratuitous blasphemy. Since bombs are your means of expression, it would be really telling if one could throw a bomb into pure mathematics. But that is impossible." (p. 23)

If the attack is on reason, the casualty is certainty. The crime is rendered more cruel by its deceptive nature, perpetrated not by those expected to attack the symbolic order, but by the keepers of the symbolic order itself. It is a crime of betrayal, by definition the hardest crime to anticipate, the hardest crime to believe, the hardest crime to accept.

"I mean to say, first, that there's but poor comfort in being able to declare that any given act of violence – damaging property or destroying life – is not the work of anarchism at all, but of something else altogether – some species of authorized scoundrelism. This, I fancy, is much more frequent than we suppose...[T]he existence of these spies amongst the revolutionary groups which we are reproached for harboring here, *does away with all certitude*" (p. 93, emphasis added).

Similarly, and around the same time, G.K. Chesterton's *The Man Who Was Thursday* (Chesterton 2007 [1908]) challenges presumptions about terrorist identities by portraying a cabal of terrorists infiltrated by counterterrorism agents to the point of excluding real terrorists, a notion that again resonates for us today. Consider how many of the FBI's successes in foiling terrorist plots were achieved against plots the Bureau itself instigated (Shipler 2012; Human Rights Watch 2014b; Greenwald and Fishman 2015b).

In October 2010, for example, David Williams, James Cromitie, Onta Williams, and Laguerre Payen – the Newburgh Four – were convicted in federal court on charges of conspiring to shoot missiles at military planes and blow up a synagogue and a Jewish Center in the Bronx, in New York City. What seemed at first blush to be a major success of the FBI's counterterrorism program turned out on closer examination to be something else entirely.

The Newburgh "terror conspiracy" began when Walmart employee James Cromitie met a man named Shahed Hussain in the parking lot of the Musjid Al-Iklhas mosque. Unbeknownst to Cromitie, Hussain was working for the FBI under threat of deportation back to Pakistan, having committed some 50 frauds (Human Rights Watch 2014a) and been busted for a scam involving drivers' licenses (The Nation 2010). Hussain had been instructed by the FBI to meet people at the mosque and get them talking about jihad.

Cromitie was a 45-year-old recovering drug addict with a history of mental disability. Hussain, on behalf of the FBI, came up with a fictional plan to fire grenades at Stewart Air Base and place bombs in a synagogue, and tried to get Cromitie involved, offering him $250,000 after he lost his job at Walmart and was in dire financial straits. Despite Hussain's best efforts at persuasion and offers of cash, Cromitie was resistant to the idea of using violence, insisting to Hussain that dying like martyrs was "not gonna change anything" (Human Rights Watch 2014a). Hussain kept after him for months, dangling the money, pushing the idea of jihad as a duty, and threatening that harm would come to him if he did not engage in the attack. Finally, the desperate Cromitie agreed to participate, on the condition that nobody would get hurt. Cromitie relayed the offer to David Williams, offering to share the money to help with his cancer-stricken brother's medical costs. The two of them invited in Onta Williams, the son of a crack-addict mother, and Laguerre Payen, a diagnosed schizophrenic who lived in an apartment strewn with bottles of urine and who thought he needed a passport to visit Florida. All four men were promised financial assistance.

In short, as US Court of Appeals Judge Reena Raggi put it: "The government came up with the crime, provided the means, and removed all relevant obstacles." The trial judge saw the case for what it was, calling Cromitie so "utterly inept" that "real terrorists would not have bothered with him" and concluding that "only the government could have made a terrorist out of Mr Cromitie, whose buffoonery is positively Shakespearean in scope." Nevertheless, she sentenced him and his three co-defendants to 25 years in prison.

The Newburgh Four case is not an isolated example. According to Human Rights Watch, since September 11, 2001 there have been some one hundred and fifty terrorism cases like this one, i.e., in which an FBI informant actively led the plotting. Typically, those drawn in and convicted are mentally and economically vulnerable people who would never have gotten involved in terrorism had they not been aggressively manipulated into some level of proximity to a fake plot.

They are people like Rezwan Ferdaus, with "obvious" mental health problems, increasingly suffering from extreme weight loss and loss of bladder control, with depression and seizures "so bad his father quit his job" to care for him; sentenced to 17 years in prison for "material support" for terrorism. Or like Mohammed Shnewer, a 19-year-old loner who persisted in arguing for nonviolent actions, prayer, and charity against an even more persistent FBI informant who continually urged him toward violence until, pressed to name a legitimate target, he named Fort Dix; he was convicted of conspiring to kill members of the US military and sentenced to life in prison. Or like Shawahar Matin Siraj, a young man with "impaired critical thinking and analytical skills" who was "more interested in cartoons than world affairs" until an FBI informant got him fired up with "grotesque pictures of abuses against Muslims"; although he "never quite agreed to the attack [planned by the FBI], saying he first had to ask his mother," he was arrested and charged with conspiring to attack a New York City subway station (Human Rights Watch 2014a).

While the oddly widespread practice of inventing terrorist plots in order to "expose" them and arrest highly manipulable mental incompetents certainly takes some of the real out of national security realism, it is not the only way the terrorism narrative suffers from fictions and ruptures. A couple of examples were covered in the chapter on dreams, for the absurd seamlessness of their discontinuities. Another one is the strange case of Abu Zubaydah.

Zubaydah was literally the man for whom US Attorney General John Yoo's famous memo justifying torture was originally written. He was, for many years, consistently described in news accounts and by multiple high-level government officials as a "top Al Qaeda lieutenant" or "al Qaeda's number two or number three guy." His capture in 2002 was big news and considered a major blow against al Qaeda. His testimony, following extensive torture and the loss of an eye, is heavily relied upon for the Al Qaeda narrative in the *9/11 Commission Report*, in which he is cited by name 52 times. Zubaydah was described as having played key operational roles in both the 1998 US embassy bombings in Africa and the 9/11 attacks. It is almost impossible to overstate how central and important Abu Zubaydah was to the story we were all told about Al Qaeda and the major terrorist attacks against the United States, and to the one we were told about why torture is justified.

Then in 2009 the US government quietly admitted in its response to a habeas corpus petition that Zubaydah had never been a member of al Qaeda, explicitly acknowledging that he had played no role in either the embassy bombings or 9/11. No changes were made to the *9/11 Commission Report* as a result of this startling disclosure, no errata were issued. No explanation was provided as to how such a massive example of misinformation became such an integral part of the story in the first place or what it implied for the reliability of the whole process and the integrity, if any, of what remained of the story. One moment Zubaydah was centrally important because of his Al Qaeda position and key involvement in its most famous attacks, and the next moment he was not. He was gone but his supposed testimony remained, unflustered. The narrative ruptured like the skin of a bubble, and then instantly resealed as if nothing had happened. Just as in a dream, the two Zubaydahs simply coexist, suspended together in an incongruous contradictory state. The physical Zubaydah remains subjected to indefinite detention at the US facility at Guantanamo (Gordon 2002; Kean and Hamilton 2004; Gates 2009; Ryan 2012). He has not been charged with any crime.

This kind of fictionalization or narrativization of reality has ripple effects on the generation and regeneration of culture and meaning. As the novelist Don DeLillo put it in *Mao II*:

> When you inflict punishment on someone who is not guilty, when you fill rooms with innocent victims, you begin to empty the world of meaning and erect a separate mental state, the mind consuming what's outside itself, replacing real things with plots and fictions. One fiction taking the world narrowly into itself, the other fiction pushing out toward the social order, trying to unfold into it. (DeLillo 1991, p. 200)

Let's take a step back, as we consider surrealism and terrorism in the context of "that sorcery-bundle of mythical representations on which Western culture is based" (Taussig 1987, p. 201), to clarify where surrealism stands in relationship to spectacular crime. As suggested in the foregoing review of surrealism's objects of fascination, the historical movement at times appeared to promote it, and in its most violent forms.

Jean Clair, the director of the Picasso museum in Paris, launched a peculiar assault on surrealism in November 2001, citing a Louis Aragon piece from 1925 as evidence that the surrealist ideology had prepared the way for the attacks of September 11 by condemning Western values and elevating those of "the Orient." Clair found echoes of the World Trade Center towers in what Aragon had written – "May faraway America collapse from all its white buildings" – and argued that violent rhetoric leads to violent actions (Eburne 2005). André Breton had faced accusations of the same kind when he wrote of the "simplest Surrealist act" of firing a gun at random into a crowd. Taken together with the surrealists' apparent celebration of murder in fiction and reality and their near-constant invocation of the language of revolution, it may indeed seem as if a call to real violence was a tenet of the movement.

If Breton's plan was to rouse people to real violence, however, it is doubtful that he'd have footnoted his notorious pronouncement about random shooting with the observation that "it is clear that my intention is not to recommend it above every other because it is simple, and to try to pick a quarrel with me on this point is tantamount to asking, in bourgeois fashion, any nonconformist why he doesn't commit suicide, or any revolutionary why he doesn't pack up and go live in the USSR" (Breton 2010 [1930], p. 126). It is more likely, then, that the surrealist interest in crime and the violent poetry of certain writers comprises its own sorcery bundle of shock value, the spirit of rebellion itself, a shaking loose of chains that allows a fresh look, a transgression of taboo to put the symbolic order on the defensive, a reckoning with the way societies produce monsters, the dark side of excessive law and order, and so forth: a bit of poetic license, in other words, rather than an unsurrealistically literal endorsement of rape, torture, and murder.

While certainly accommodating similar concerns, the emphasis of a surrealist mode of inquiry in the present context is also substantially different. What we have here is not a provocative celebration or aesthetic quasi-justification of undisputed acts of terrorism, but a deep dive into its discursive "phantasmagoria." To be sure, the socioeconomic and geopolitical factors of how and why terrorists are produced, the beyond-language measures resorted to by the voiceless, the cynical amplification of favored jihadists and mercenaries for strategic ends, the strangely symbiotic media-terrorism relationship, and the power relationships that determine who gets to call whom a terrorist are all ripe for exploration in a surrealist mode. Beyond those things, however, terrorism invites surrealist inquiry along epistemological lines: inquiry into paranoia, dreamlike discontinuities, narratives built on unreliable assumptions, the expansion of an authoritarian quasi-fascism in the name of counterterrorism, the murky, shifting unrealities of intelligence operations.

The most salient aspect of all this for present purposes is the reality-shaping power of terrorism discourse itself, with all its "referential invalidity" and "rhetorical circularity" (Douglass and Zulaika 1996, p. ix) as well as outright deception and invention. Undermining the credibility of that discourse is an essential part of our project to take the real out of national security realism. As we have seen, nowhere is the problematic intermingling of fiction and fact more evident than in the thoroughly mediated and intelligence-agency-dependent world of terrorism narrative.

Terrorism is spectacle. From the invention of dynamite and the introduction of the invisible attacker, problems of identity have been at the heart of terrorism discourse. One of the implications of the identity problematic is that it leaves enormous space for the free floating of untethered signifiers, the endless dreamy shifting of meanings and characterizations, until ultimately we confront "the radical extent to which terrorism discourse constitutes its object" (Douglass and Zulaika 1996, p. 16).

For starters the term is famously difficult to define. The League of Nations and the United Nations both tried and failed to come up with a definition that was acceptable to all and could hold states accountable; there were too many concerns about what constituted justification and the implication of those who wanted to do the implicating. Terrorism is such a slippery category that Sean McBride, Menachem Begin, Yassir Arafat, and Nelson Mandela all went from being considered terrorists to being winners of the Nobel Peace Prize. Iran, Iraq, and Syria have all shifted back and forth from being blacklisted as terrorism supporters to being allies of the West. Meanwhile Saudi Arabia has consistently remained an ally despite having been identified, without controversy, as "the world's largest source of funds for Islamist militant groups" (Walsh 2010), and the West supports, perhaps creates, groups like Al Nusra in Syria or Al Qaeda in Afghanistan when it suits geopolitical ambition. Clearly, the designation is subject to the vagaries and conveniences of political considerations, which is why the discourse is its own object; there is nothing outside that text.

It only gets murkier from there. The intelligence-terrorism world is populated by people like Ali Mohamed, who simultaneously works for the CIA, serves as an FBI informant, is an instructor for the US Army at the John F. Kennedy Special Warfare School at Fort Bragg, is a close confidant of Osama Bin Laden, trains mujahideen in Afghanistan and Somalia, establishes Al Qaeda cells in Santa Clara, California, and Nairobi, Kenya, and trains most of the 1993 World Trade Center bombers at the Al-Kifah Refugee Center in Brooklyn. The US is aware of all these activities, and Mohamed even details it over dinner for some FBI agents and US Prosecutor Patrick Fitzgerald, who were seeking his cooperation. Mohamed rejects the cooperation but is not arrested at that time. He is eventually arrested and pleads guilty in connection with the 1998 embassy bombings planned out of his Nairobi cell, but is never sentenced. His wife says: "They have Ali pretty secretive...it's like he just kinda vanished into thin air." (History Commons undated-a)

The intelligence-terrorism world is also populated by people like Anwar Al-Awlaki, known mainly for being the first US citizen to be killed by an executive-decreed drone strike without being charged with a crime or otherwise permitted due process. Al-Awlaki led a complicated existence, being simultaneously a close associate of several suspects in multiple terrorist attacks and the toast of the town in Washington DC.

The FBI opened an investigation on him in 1999 for his ties to Osama bin Laden. He was the "spiritual advisor" to future alleged 9/11 hijackers Nawaf Alhazmi, Khalid Almihdhar, and Hani Hanjour; he talked a lot on the phone with Omar al-Bayoumi, a suspected Saudi intelligence officer who helped Alhazmi and Almihdhar in San Diego (History Commons undated-b). Alhazmi and Almihdhar, incidentally, lived in San Diego with an FBI informant, and had been on the CIA's radar since attending an Al Qaeda summit meeting in Malaysia in January 2000 (Vries 2002). According to Major General Abdul Qadir al-Shami, the deputy-head of the Yemeni Security and Intelligence Service, Al-Awlaki was arrested in Yemen for involvement in the bombing of the USS Cole, but was released by request of CIA Director George Tenet in 2001, who said "this is my person, this is my problem, this is my issue…The man must be released." (Rubinstein 2021.)

Despite being under FBI investigation for suspicion of links with Al Qaeda, he was able to travel freely between the US, the UK, and Yemen. Contradicting FBI denials, a FOIA request shows the FBI possessed credit card records showing that Al-Awlaki purchased plane tickets for three of the alleged 9/11 hijackers. Perhaps the FBI denied it because in the immediate aftermath of 9/11, Al-Awlaki was "one of Washington DC's go-to Muslim sources," considered a moderate voice, leading prayer services in the US Capitol and attending luncheons with senior military officials at the Pentagon.

In 2002, he was detained upon entering the US, either because he was on the terrorist watch list (History Commons undated-b) or because there was an arrest warrant for passport fraud (Rubinstein 2021), but was quickly released either because he had been taken off the watch list the day before (History Commons undated-b) or because a federal judge rescinded the arrest warrant the very same day (Rubinstein 2021). He was arrested in Yemen again in 2006, this time for involvement in an Al Qaeda plot to kidnap a US military attaché, only to be released once again at the behest of US officials (Rubinstein 2021). In 2011 his peculiar career was ended by a CIA drone strike.

I offer these stories – and there are many more just like them – not to posit any conspiracy theories nor indeed to venture any attempt at deciphering any meaning at all, but rather specifically to highlight the difficulty of assigning meaning. Agents, double agents, blowback, plots: who on earth knows what's going on? Even CIA agents must get confused at times! What we have here are consummate examples of Taussig's "epistemic murk." When Jean Baudrillard describes a world that "can no longer dream" because images have become indistinguishable from the real "as though things had swallowed their own mirrors" (2008, p. 4), or when Louis Aragon states that "[t]he only way to look at Man is as the victim of his mirrors" (2010 [1924]), they weren't speaking about the mystifying interplay of intelligence and terrorism, but they might as well have been. Baudrillard's notion of simulacra and hyperreality have real resonance in this context, one-upping the surrealists "by locating the unreal 'in the real's hallucinatory resemblance to itself'" (San Juan Jr. 2004, p. 124).

This is the stuff from which national security states are built: so what is this stuff? For a surrealist mode of inquiry, these are not only cautionary tales against certainty, but invitations to query why so much taboo is associated with questioning a state of affairs that is so patently questionable.

Chapter 5

Black Humor

"Whenever he makes a joke, there is always a problem hidden inside."
Goethe, speaking about Georg Lichtenberg, as quoted by André
Breton in the Anthology of Black Humour (2009 [1997], p. 60)

"What a way to start the week!"
Condemned man being led to the gallows on a Monday,
in   Freud's   example   of   humor   in   service   of
the   ego,   as   related   by   André   Breton   in   the
Anthology of Black Humour (2009 [1997], p. 24)

The best argument for black humor being a signature element
of surrealism, apart from its self-evidence in surrealist works, is
André Breton's decision to publish an *Anthology of Black Humour*
(2009 [1997]) as part of his canon. Breton does not offer a precise
definition of black humor in the *Anthology*. The closest he comes is
to say that black humor "is the mortal enemy of sentimentality...
and of a certain short-lived whimsy" (p. 25) and to note that
"Mexico...with its splendid funeral toys, stands as the chosen
land of black humour" (p. 23). Speaking of humor generally,
Breton quotes (with reservations) Louis Aragon's appropriately
surreal but strictly "external" definition: "Humour is what
soup, chickens and symphony orchestras lack" (p. 22). Breton
himself prefers a more inward-focused view of humor as "a
superior revolt of the mind" (p. 22).

Black humor, it seems to me, is what happens when absurdity
meets the void. The best way to ruin humor is to analyze it, but
with that risk in mind, this is a complex form of humor that
can be simultaneously funny and not funny. Its comedic power
derives from finding incongruities or speaking the unspoken in

things that are no laughing matter. Its affinity with surrealism is grounded in their shared gravitation toward the tabooed and the tapping of illicit or unconscious truths. It defies the void by reasserting humanity in the face of meaningless nothingness, making it, perhaps counterintuitively, a determinedly optimistic form of humor, but it is as likely to evoke a chill as laughter.

In his introduction to Jonathan Swift's entry in the anthology, Breton identifies Swift as the "true initiator" of black humor, as "a man who...was constantly outraged [and who]...'provokes laughter, but does not share in it'" (Breton 2009 [1997], p. 29). Breton argues that Swift was able to "externalize the sublime" and thereby "transcend the merely comic" (Breton 2009 [1997], p. 30). The modifier "black" implies a dark counterbalance to any levity, and black humor can contain so much bitterness or horror that it "need not be 'funny,' in the usual sense of the word" (Rosemont 1989b, p. 84), even when it provokes laughter. Black humor, for Breton, is "a complicated combination of Hegel's poetic 'objective humour' [*Objektiverhumor*] and Freud's ironic 'gallows humour' [*Galgenhumor*]" (Haynes 2006, p. 25). The Freudian aspect may reflect black humor's use as a tool of psychological liberation, but in its Hegelian aspect it performs a "dialectical turn [and] becomes the articulation of a kind of 'social unconscious'" (Haynes 2006, p. 26). It is "a discursive weapon to contest symbolically the dominant discourse of society" (Erickson 1988, p. 199). Black humor reveals "foreign bodies" in our unconscious and can exploit the tension between what the big Other knows and what we know but may not yet consciously acknowledge.

The wider and deeper the breach between the official and the unofficial conscious, the more difficult it becomes for motives of inner speech to turn into outward speech... wherein they might acquire formulation, clarity and rigor. Motives under these conditions begin to fail, to lose their verbal countenance, and little by little really do turn into a 'foreign body' in the psyche (Haynes 2006, p. 37, quoting Vološinov on Freud within discussion of black humor).

The social and political nature of surrealism's use of black humor and its relevance to the notion of the big Other derives from the realization that "black humour points up a foreignness not on the peripheries of social discourse but right at its 'official' centre" (Haynes 2006, p. 37). Breton's thinking about surrealist black humor was strongly influenced by Jacques Vaché and his concept of "Umour" – a "sensation...of the theatrical (and joyless) pointlessness of everything" (Ristić 2015 [1933], p. 200) – which, again, effectively had the big Other in its sights as the prime target. For Vaché, Umour was a strategy to be employed against the "debraining machine," a concept borrowed from Alfred Jarry and representing official social discourse's way of "depriving human beings of the ability to think and dream for themselves" (Rosemont 2008, p. 71).

Proulx, Heine *et al* (2010) have argued that absurdist black humor, such as in Kafka's parable *An Imperial Message* or the Monty Python treatment of *Biggles: Pioneer Air Fighter*, can create an "unfamiliar familiar" resulting in a sense of the uncanny that threatens and disturbs people's "meaning frameworks." As the authors note, absurdist humor, unlike standard jokes that resolve incongruities into a kind of sense, "does not culminate in a punch line that restores meaning" (p. 821), but instead multiplies the incongruities with a relentlessly destabilizing effect. Thus this kind of humor, particularly of the black variety, serves the essential surrealist goal of provoking a *crise de conscience* (Breton 2010 [1930], p. 123) – sometimes translated as crisis of consciousness and sometimes as attack of conscience – why not both simultaneously?

Humor in this vein is effective not only because of its inherent positive qualities, but because without it a transgressive political argument may well suffer from a strident polemicism. In short, without humor, surrealism is insufferable. There is an enormous difference between someone insisting that your reality is delusional while angrily slamming her hand on the table, and someone insisting that your reality is delusional with a smile and a twinkle in her eye. A touch of humor, perhaps especially black humor, is the best indicator imaginable that an interlocutor speaking of dreams, paranoia, and terrorism is not mad. Style, as we know from the chapter on paranoia, is everything. An effective antidote to the paranoid style is the blackly humorous style.

One of the reasons to employ black humor in a mode of inquiry that hopes to multiply political uncertainties – i.e., one of the reasons it is able to provoke a crisis – is that it is not subject to rational counter-argument or any of the other usual forms of intellectual resistance. It connects the conscious to the unconscious.

> Attempts to achieve [a shift in consciousness] by "serious," rational means invariably prove self-defeating. Rational argument affects only a very small number of people a very small part of the time...People who *consciously* respect the police, admire their employer, and revere the church fathers nonetheless will laugh heartily at film comedies, songs and comic strips that sadistically ridicule cops, bosses, and preachers. The "comic situation" allows the unconscious truth to erupt into consciousness in a spontaneously liberating way. (Rosemont 1989b, p. 83)

Humor – black, absurdist humor – is a key tactic within the strategy of a surrealist mode of inquiry. It's not an argument, it makes no claims, and as such is irrefutable. It entertains and disturbs "meaning frameworks" by an illicit appeal to that which people can know and the big Other cannot. Black humor is a joke at the big Other's expense. Every joke, as George Orwell said, is a tiny revolution (Orwell 1968).

Black humor can be discussed in terms of the theory of a surrealist mode of inquiry but it's also key to the practice of what is essentially an artistic approach to political analysis or activism. Without claiming that the following examples must only be seen as exhibiting a surrealist mode of art – they can all be described in various other ways as well – we can nevertheless appeal to artistic efforts that draw from the surrealist toolkit: dreaminess, anti-fascism, crime, paranoia, black humor.

Flann O'Brien's *The Third Policeman* is a dreamlike crime novel whose absurdist comedy underscores rather than undermines its seriousness because of the book's black heart: the murder that serves as its inciting incident. The crime is described in the sort of horrific detail that ensures it can never be left behind by the reader. With something so grievous as ballast, no matter how absurd the text gets it never becomes light. On the contrary, the more the narrative amuses the more it simultaneously frightens, tethered, as it were, to a corpse. This is a disturbing and potent combination of forces. The horror would not be as solemn, nor the humor as exhilarating, did they not occur together in this juxtaposition. The combination of the comic and the horrific, not as poles in opposition but as the razor's edge between, gives black humor its destabilizing power. By "capitalizing on the traumas of the external world...as an occasion for pleasure" (Erickson 1988, p. 208), black humor defeats our resistance to being disturbed.

As in *The Third Policeman*, the extravagant levity of Leonora Carrington's *The Hearing Trumpet* successfully avoids flying away on its own ebullience by virtue of the sober reality at the heart of it. For O'Brien it was murder; for Carrington, it is the prospect of its protagonist's senility and her family's decision, having had enough of her, to put her conveniently out of sight. This is the sort of solemn narrative detail that tolls like a funeral bell throughout regardless of what else happens. Carrington is free to pursue her imagination's fancies wherever they lead without her story losing its heart. Some of the funniest and most absurd lines also contain the darkest sense of menace: "She nodded gravely and pointed into the soup with the long wooden spoon. 'Jump into the broth, meat is scarce this season.'" (Carrington 2005 [1974], p. 138.) Or: "Audrey was found congealed upside-down in a small iceberg that invaded her bedroom. She was still holding an empty bottle of champagne to her lips." (p. 153.)

A similar phenomenon occurs in Boris Vian's *Froth on the Daydream*. On the one hand the book feels as whimsical and frothy as the title implies but, like *The Third Policeman* and *The Hearing Trumpet*, there is a seriousness at its center, in this case a melancholy sense of futility. Protagonist Colin's love, Chloe, is afflicted with a water-lily on the lung and he gladly depletes his fortune to buy her the flowers that seem to help. A "remedy shop" is full of machines, one of which hides under its rusty tin cover "a composite animal, half-flesh, half-metal...killing itself swallowing the basic materials and expulsing them in the form of little round pills." (p. 121.) Nor is he able to save Chloe, in the end. She dies, and her body "disappears." The household becomes so gloomy that a resident mouse decides to commit suicide by making an agreement with a reluctant cat: the mouse will put its head in the cat's mouth; the cat will stretch out its tail; as soon as someone steps on the tail, the cat will involuntarily decapitate the mouse. The mouse's head goes in and they wait on the pavement, the cat's tail outstretched, awaiting the fatal step. Eleven little girls from an orphanage are heard getting nearer: "They were singing. And they were blind." (p. 221.) This is how the novel ends, simultaneously hilarious and heart-breaking – a beautiful effect that is in large part enabled by the dreamlike strategy of a surrealist literary mode.

In *El Señor Presidente* (Asturias 1980 [1946]), name-checked by Deleuze in his article on the philosophy of Duhamel's *Série*

Noire crime series, Miguel Angel Asturias uses a particularly relentless and poetic form of writing that can be called black humor. It is of the type that provokes little laughter, so infused is it with violence and terror. Indeed the text is so unfunny that it initially seems odd to call it humor at all, regardless of how black. Yet outwardly it bears a resemblance to comedy, maintaining a certain carnivalesque sensibility somehow, as if the narrative had the form of a farce into which something horrific had been poured. Asturias's novel, which won him the 1967 Nobel Prize in Literature, has been variously described as "the first fully-fledged Surrealist novel in Latin America" (Martin 1989, p. 149), as an early example of magic realism, and as a bridge between European surrealism and Latin American magic realism (ibid). It has a dreamlike quality throughout.

"I have been informed both by the cook in that house (who was spying on her master and the housemaid) and the housemaid (who was spying on her master and the cook), that Angel Face was shut in his room with General Canales for approximately three-quarters of an hour." (p. 65.)

"His laughter hardened in his mouth like the plaster dentists use for their models." (p. 49.)

The bitter observations and the startling imagery create a tone that is at once comic and unnerving, a powerful entry into the world of black humor via small absurd details, such as a terrified man suddenly shaken by hiccups. Asturias manages an artful balancing act, in which everything feels like some sort of macabre puppet show – an actual puppeteer figures prominently – brimming with a menacing nonchalance that seems simultaneously to amuse and accuse. A pitiful aid to the president, an essentially comic figure in his tremulous impotence, enters as if to a vague expectation of slapstick, only to be taken away for a punishment of 200 lashes for tipping over an inkwell. The president is informed over his dinner that the man was unable to withstand the lashes and has died, to which he responds: "Well, what of it? Bring the next course!" (p. 36.)

Later in the novel, the puppeteer Don Benjamin, "hardly three feet tall and as slender and hairy as a bat," inspired by a shooting that occurred outside his home, decides to incorporate some tragedy into his children's productions. He designs a way for his puppets to cry.

> Don Benjamin thought that the painful element in the drama would make the children cry, and his surprise knew no bounds when he saw them laugh more heartily than before, with wide open mouths and happy expressions. The sight of tears made the children laugh. The sight of blows made the children laugh. (p. 54)

Numerous other examples could be drawn from cinema. Terry Gilliam's *Brazil* springs to mind, with its Monty Python-esque sense of the comically absurd put to use in service of an anti-fascist sensibility. While it has been described as a "satire on bureaucratic society" (Street 2009) – which it certainly is, in part – it is the way the inhuman bureaucracy supports totalitarian surveillance, torture, and abuse of the concept of terrorism that is the real source of the film's paranoid horror. Delusion figures prominently as well, not least in the ending sequence where we discover that what at first appeared to be a dramatic escape from the torturer's chair into freedom and happiness is instead only the fantasy of the now-lobotomized protagonist. Throughout the proceedings, plastic surgery-obsessed characters literally attempt to put a superficial happy-face on their outlook to increasingly grotesque, and horrifyingly comic, effect.

Humor has long been employed for its effectiveness in communicating incongruity, hypocrisy, and injustice. The darker the target, the blacker the humor. This strategic use of humor can simultaneously provoke laughter and outrage, while demonstrating an inherent optimism or vitality of the human spirit even in the midst of the most cynical acknowledgment of the most repressive political currents. Humor's exploitation of incongruity, or the jarring juxtaposition of ideas, harmonizes perfectly with the strategies of a surrealist mode of inquiry. The usefulness of this humor in this regard has not been lost on social movements and political activist organizations.

The Guerrilla Girls, not unlike the Guerrilla Art Action Group (GAAG) before them, were an artist-activist collective dedicated to subverting certain cultural norms of the official art world as represented by major galleries and museums, which they felt reproduced gender and class inequalities of society at large. Both groups adopted an approach that involved "bringing the arts into the streets" (Hendricks and Toche 1978). While the GAAG emphasized their own subversive radicalism with a certain stridency, the Guerrilla Girls emphasized humor in their approach "as a deliberate strategic choice" (Leng 2020) because of their power to disrupt hegemonic worldviews. Their posters highlighting statistics about representation in the art world did more than make intellectual arguments; they "made it seem absolutely ridiculous that white men should monopolize gallery space" and the other institutions of "good art" (ibid).

There are obviously innumerable other examples. The performance artist-activist Reverend Billy assumes a persona that's a sort of Day-Glo mash-up of an evangelical preacher and Elvis Presley, taking to the streets of New York City alone or with his Church of Stop Shopping choir to perform, for example, exorcisms at Starbucks franchises or big banks, or to proclaim insistently at the Disney Store in Times Square that Mickey Mouse is the anti-Christ. Part of the fascination of the Reverend Billy character, invented and performed by Bill Talen, is that it isn't simply satire; Talen appropriates the forms and gestures of the preacher and inhabits them to preach a very real anti-consumerist, environment-friendly message whose comic sensibilities are matched by the genuine fervor of the delivery.

Upon one's first encounter with Reverend Billy, one is likely to spend much of the time wondering: is this guy for real?

The Yes Men, pranksters extraordinaire, impersonate powerful government or corporate entities and promote either openly horrific plans or extravagantly decent ones. For example, posing as a Dow Chemical spokesman after the chemical disaster in Bhopal, one of the Yes Men appeared on the BBC World News and claimed that Dow planned to liquidate Union Carbide and use the 12 billion dollars in proceeds to pay for victims' medical care, site clean-up, and research into eliminating the hazards of other Dow products. For about 2 hours this news was considered real, and one immediate effect was a 2-billion-dollar drop in Dow's stock market value (Graff 2004). When Dow repudiated the story and emphasized that it would do no such thing, the company was rewarded with a rebound of its market value. Thus the Yes Men shone a light not only on Dow's abrogation of social responsibility, but also on the perversities of incentives in capitalism (to say nothing of the fact-checking procedures at major news institutions).

In a similar spirit, the Billionaires for Bush attended numerous rallies against then-President George W. Bush, dressed in tuxedos, drinking champagne, and "defending" their president's billionaire-favoring policies; Target Ain't People sprang a flashmob protest in August 2010, "singing and dancing their critique of corporate personhood and Target's financial support of an anti-gay politician" (Kutz-Flamenbaum 2014); Adbusters regularly practices a kind of satirical culture jamming, for example with its image of the US flag with corporate logos in place of the stars; the Raging Grannies, in their guise as stereotypical harmless little old ladies, sing their scathing critiques of political corruption to the tune of American folk standards.

The inclusion of humor in activism is not the sole purview of comfortable middle-class protesters. The Zapatistas, a group of anti-globalization and land-reform activists in southern Mexico, often use humor in framing their agenda in their documents and in speeches. Subcomandante Marcos humorously retells, for example, how the original Zapatista urban intellectual "illuminati" from Mexico City were schooled by the indigenous communities of Chiapas. The comical narrative serves the dual purpose of revealing the flawed, human side of the originators, making the group more easily relatable to outsiders, and instructing us as to where the real leadership is and must be: directly from the people suffering most from the policies they're trying to reform. Marcos also tells a very funny story about a chicken among the Zapatistas who, in trying to walk like a man to avoid being eaten, looked like a penguin, provoking both laughter and sympathy and succeeding in its quest for survival. Having elicited laughter from the tale, he draws an analogy to the plight of the Zapatistas themselves, the element of humor making his point both more poignant and more effective (Olesen 2007).

Ebenezer Obadare describes how essential humor is as an element of "infrapolitics" in Nigeria, a below-the-radar realm of political activity embedded in culture. Against a backdrop of nominally democratic post-military regimes that nonetheless replicate many of the practices and norms of the previous, openly autocratic, era, a style of humor emerges as both critique and coping mechanism in the context of "a reality that is decidedly surreal" (Obadare 2009). Typically jokes circulate impugning either particular authority figures or a more generalized lamenting of the "state of things" in the nation. Hell figures in many of them. One example features a man who goes to hell and finds it divided by nation. One by one he visits the German hell, the American hell, the Russian hell, and discovers that they all involve time in an electric chair, a bed of nails, and copious whipping.

Then he comes to the Nigerian hell and finds that there is a very long line of people waiting to get in. Amazed, he asks, "What do they do here?" He is told, "First they put you in an electric chair for an hour. Then they lay you on a bed of nails for another hour. Then the Nigerian devil comes in and whips you for the rest of the day."

"But that is exactly the same as all other hells – why are there so many people waiting to get in?" "Because there is never any electricity, so the electric chair does not work; someone stole all the nails; and the devil used to be a public servant, so he comes in, punches his timecard, and then goes back home." (ibid)

Black humor doesn't get any blacker than comic work produced in Nazi concentration camps. Gurs was the largest concentration camp in occupied France, and something of a hotbed of artistic resistance. Horst Rosenthal was an artist who left behind two graphic novels depicting daily life in Gurs with powerful humor and irony. One has Mickey Mouse as its protagonist, and is full of humorous cartoon images along with "amusing and 'childish' texts" that "stand in sharp contrast to the harsh reality of the camp" (Rosenberg 2002). Similarly, political prisoners in the Gulag left behind a memoir literature that is rich in humor that documents, critiques, and resists within "a context of dislocation and horror" (Belokowsky 2019).

The very fact that people can respond in this manner not only *to* the worst and most brutal circumstances imaginable but *in the midst* of them is in itself a defiant and profound statement of the power of the human spirit to resist, as well as proof of the essential role humor plays in dark times. Whether used in political art or activism or just as a form of permission we can give ourselves, alone or as a means of social bonding, to break tension with laughter, black humor is about as fine a communications tool as there is, and it provides a crucial psychological defense against the madness of the times. Its employment within a surrealist mode of inquiry makes potentially esoteric critical concerns more accessible, bypasses intellectual defense mechanisms that make us resistant to seeing things in a new way, and does the performative surrealist work of stimulating the connections between our conscious and unconscious minds.

Conclusion

[The surrealists] sought not so much to convince as to move, not so much to argue the cause of a particular program as to arouse the feeling of revolt and to prompt the demand that something *must be done. While the Communists instructed the proletariat in the strategy of revolution, the Surrealists were trying to bring about the emotional climate in which the revolution might break out.*
Robert Short, The Politics of Surrealism, 1920-1936 (2003, p. 27)

Balzac was the first to speak of the ruins of the bourgeoisie. But it was Surrealism that first opened our eyes to them.
Walter Benjamin, Paris, Capital of the Nineteenth Century (1999 [1935], p. 13)

This book's central ideas all have to do with words that are notoriously hard to define: surrealism; reality; fascism; terrorism; insanity. With each additional layer of elusive abstraction, the fuzziness of the whole panoply multiplies. Ambiguities and flexibilities abound, and boundaries exist only to be tested. Have we ended up with anything more than a meaningless (or mean-anything) hodgepodge of fatally vague notions? What can we conclude from this eclectic collection of slippery concepts in wobbly orbit around our proposed mode of querying the national security state?

For starters, we've seen that the ontological givens offered of a discourse, particularly including that of the national security state, are subject to any number of contingencies that expose the fictive elements of the putative real. We've acknowledged that the border between dreamwork and presumptive reality is generous and permeable in both directions. We've looked closely enough at the nexus of intelligence, terrorism, and disinformation to see it in all of its unreliable "epistemic murk" – certainly enough, at a minimum, not to put all of our confidence in the official representations of the big Other. In short, a surrealist mode of inquiry begins with a great refusal: a refusal to accept in a facile way the realism of realpolitik. A surrealist mode of inquiry sees the fictions, lives the dream, and wants to know: where are all these elaborations of the national security state taking us?

It is, to say the least, difficult to view one's own culture in one's own moment with the kind of detached analytical perspective that comes relatively easily with time or distance. Just as we can so often see flaws in other people more easily than we can in ourselves, or see what we should have done differently 10 or 20 years ago, so it is with cultures. Distant cultures and distant times are whole forests, substantially disinvested of our own identities; the present moment is thick with individual trees growing out of the soil of who we are now. Of course, we have criticisms of our own contemporary politics and culture, but it's not so easy from close up to see it in its systemic entirety, with the full weight of the big Other against us.

Part of the job of a surrealist mode of inquiry, then, is to develop the superpower of seeing the "here and now" as if it were "there" or "then." Combining an awareness of unconscious biases, the intermingling of fact, fiction, dream, delusion, and socialization in the cultural narrative, with a keen sensitivity to Ur-fascist developments and an even keener sense of humor, a surrealist mode of inquiry proceeds by interrogating every positive assertion and negative taboo that serves to uphold the symbolic order of the national security state. Once again, as Mark Fisher observed, the best hope for resistance to capitalist realism's claims to inevitability is to show that its "ostensible realism is nothing of the sort" (Fisher 2009, p. 16). If capitalist realism and its national security dependencies have long since "colonized the dreaming life of the population" (ibid, p. 9), a surrealist mode of inquiry is an anti-colonialist revolution to reclaim dreamwork.

It is as much a personal effort as a political one. A surrealist mode of inquiry must look within as well as without, in order to locate the internalized obstacles to imaginative and analytical freedom. It's useless to recognize half the world's propagandists, for example, if we remain in the thrall of the other half. It's easy for the left to see through right-wing rhetoric, and vice versa. It's substantially harder to see how your own "side" is being managed, bounded, and used, but this is what is required in order to access the meta-level of a political system. This process of checking ourselves is continual in a surrealist mode of inquiry, in order to ensure we settle for neither the smug critiques of the most antithetical political party nor the empty rhetoric of the least objectionable. This is not a partisan exercise. The lowest level of critical thinking is picking out deceit, hypocrisy, and baseless assumptions among the politicians we despise the most. A higher level is doing the same to the ones we want to like. The highest level is doing it to ourselves. It should be an uncomfortable process. If it's comfortable, we're not doing it right.

Yet it's not as simple as burning the newspaper, throwing the television out of the window, and rejecting everything as dubious lies or declaring everything unknowable either – although a surrealist could probably do worse. Recognizing that the processes of paranoid delusion and ordinary socialization are fundamentally similar or that "the normal are not detectably sane" (Rosenhan 1973) does not mean that there's no such thing as mental health. A surrealist mode of inquiry may be less interested in getting a grip on reality than in loosening reality's grip on us, but it doesn't recommend losing your mind and drifting off into a lonely netherworld where nothing is true, nothing is real, and there's nobody left to laugh with.

It's important to note that a surrealist mode of inquiry is a way of thinking; it does not prescribe a particular set of beliefs.

For example, its acknowledgment that officially sanctioned conspiracy theories do not necessarily enjoy evidentiary superiority over their tabooed cousins requires neither the acceptance nor the rejection of any particular theory or class of theory. It only requires a certain skepticism, deriving from alertness to the interplay of dreamwork and the big Other, wielded playfully and with incisive humor. The playfulness of the mindset does not make it frivolous; rather it fosters that healthy combination of agility, imagination, and discernment that are our most dependable allies in resisting the sort of nonsense that Ur-fascists are likely to try to foist on us.

This kind of critical distance is a fundamental necessity for the appreciation of the common ground shared by history and fiction. Novelists and historians perform functions that are formally similar: "the process of fusing events, whether imaginary or real, into a comprehensible totality capable of serving as the *object* of a representation is a poetic process" (White 1985 [1978], p. 125). The process of ordering, of crafting something coherent out of the chaos of the real, means there is authorship. Authorship of history, including history as recent as today's headlines, means that the storyteller's constraints and biases – conscious and unconscious, personal and institutional – are as important as the narrative details.

While these are paranoid times and we employ paranoia as a conceptual tool – and there is no shortage of propaganda and duplicity in the information ecosystem – the notion of authorship and fictive history doesn't exclusively imply intentional deception. As Noam Chomsky pointed out in response to a journalist's objection to Chomsky and Herman's propaganda model of media (2002 [1988]): "I'm not saying you're self-censoring. I'm sure you believe everything you're saying. But what I'm saying is that if you believed something different, you wouldn't be sitting where you're sitting" (Marr 1996). As compelling as all paranoid and tabooed subjects are for a surrealist mode of inquiry, it's neither necessary nor advisable to posit conspiracy as the sole driver of the various ways the narratives of the symbolic order are disseminated and maintained.

The question must be asked, given the tense juxtaposition of surveillance state national security paranoia with our cultural self-image as the defenders of democracy and civil rights; given the climate of fake news and alternative facts; given that dissent outside of narrow strictures has been driven out of our dreams; given that black humor is a light in dark times: is there a mode of inquiry out there more suitable to the present historical moment? I mean take a look around. You've got to admit: the world, in case you hadn't noticed, has gone a bit surreal lately.

Endnotes

Introduction

1. Lacan was "greatly influenced by [the surrealists'] writings on psychoanalysis and paranoia" (James 2009, p. 54), and his first published work appeared in the surrealist journal *Minotaure* (Lacan 1933).

Chapter 2

1. Recall that the symbolic order should not be confused even with openly stated actual policy. The former is more than capable of maintaining its official antipathy toward neo-Nazis while the latter supports them in, for example, Ukraine (Parry 2015). This is the sort of jarring juxtaposition, replete with dreamlike discontinuity, that draws the surrealist gaze in the first place.

2. Whitehead focuses on heavy-handed law enforcement themes, such as the use of no-knock SWAT team raids against suspected nonviolent drug offenders, sometimes resulting in innocent people (and pets) being shot with impunity.

3. Wolf's ten steps to fascism are: 1) invoke a terrifying internal and external enemy; 2) create secret prisons; 3) develop a thug caste; 4) set up internal surveillance; 5) harass citizens' groups; 6) engage in arbitrary detention and release; 7) target key individuals; 8) control the press; 9) equate dissent with treason; 10) suspend the rule of law. She reckons we're on step 10.

4. Wolin's "inverted" totalitarianism is an authoritarian surveillance society that is systemic rather than dependent upon a single charismatic leader, deriving power and legitimacy from multiple ideologically attuned cultural institutions, creating an apathetic and demobilized

population rather than an actively mobilized one, while asserting an external threat in order to maintain a state of emergency.

5.   Starting with the Patriot Act will, if nothing else, save time and skip us at least into the present millennium, since the abuses of Project Paperclip, which included the US building an intelligence apparatus with Nazi war criminals (Wala 2016), and COINTELPRO, which included the murder of Black Panther leader Fred Hampton (Taylor 2014), may seem too distant to have sufficient relevance today – although a continuity certainly exists and can be traced.

6.   In 2003, a young woman called Nayirah tearfully told the Congressional Human Rights Caucus a story of Iraqi soldiers ripping babies out of incubators in a Kuwaiti hospital and heaving them onto the cold floor to die. Her testimony was false. She turned out to be the daughter of the Kuwait ambassador to the US, and the incubator story was part of a propaganda campaign devised by Hill & Knowlton for its Kuwaiti client, an organization that wanted the US to invade Iraq. The testimony was even initially verified by Amnesty International, which somehow added a number for effect: 312 infants died after being removed from incubators by Iraqi soldiers, the organization reported (Jamieson and Waldman 2003, p. 16). The number was made up, the story was an invention from start to finish, and Amnesty eventually retracted its verification, but the PR exercise had its desired effect: shortly thereafter, by five votes in the Senate, the US Congress voted to go to war in Iraq. The incubator story had received major media play and been cited numerous times by President Bush and on the Senate floor (Mickey 1997), and "was a major factor in building public backing for war" (Rowse 1992).

7.   The characterizations themselves are demonstrably inaccurate. Henderson and Whelan were both integral to

the investigation, senior investigators with impeccable credentials in leadership positions, as voluminous evidence demonstrates (Wikileaks 2019; Mate 2020c; Mate 2020b; Mate 2020a). Among their supporters was José Bustani, the first Director-General of the OPCW, who stated his opinion that they had presented "convincing evidence of irregular behavior" that was "very disturbing" (Mate 2020a).

References

Abramson, Kate, 2014. "Turning up the Lights on Gaslighting." *Philosophical Perspectives* **28** (1): 1-30.

ACLU, 2009. *Reclaiming Patriotism: A Call to Reconsider the Patriot Act*. New York: American Civil Liberties Union. March 2009. https://www.aclu.org/sites/default/files/pdfs/safefree/patriot_report_20090310.pdf

ACLU, undated-a. "How the USA PATRIOT Act Redefines 'Domestic Terrorism'." Retrieved April 8, 2017, from https://www.aclu.org/other/how-usa-patriot-act-redefines-domestic-terrorism.

ACLU, undated-b. *More About Joint Terrorism Task Forces*. American Civil Liberties Union. https://www.aclu.org/other/more-about-joint-terrorism-task-forces

ACLU, undated-c. *Surveillance Under the Patriot Act*. American Civil Liberties Union. https://www.aclu.org/issues/national-security/privacy-and-surveillance/surveillance-under-patriot-act

Adorno, Theodor, 1991 [1956]. Looking Back On Surrealism. *Notes to Literature (European Perspectives: A Series in Social Thought and Cultural Criticism)*. New York: Columbia University Press. **1**: 86-90.

Ahmed, Nafeez Mossadeq, 2015. "The Circus: How British Intelligence Primed Both Sides of the 'Terror War'." *Middle East Eye*. February 27, 2015. http://www.middleeasteye.net/columns/circus-how-british-intelligence-primed-both-sides-terror-war-55293733

Alexander, Bryant Keith and Jamar Myers-Montgomery, 2016. "Militarized Police and Unpermitted Protest." *Cultural Studies* ↔ *Critical Methodologies* **16** (3): 278-286.

Allegretti, Aubrey and Maya Wolfe-Robinson, 2021. "New Anti-Protest Bill Raises Profound Concern and Alarm, Human Rights Groups Say." *The Guardian*. March 14, 2021. https://www.theguardian.com/uk-news/2021/mar/14/new-anti-protest-bill-raises-profound-concern-human-rights-groups-say

Aragon, Louis, 2010 [1924]. *A Wave of Dreams*. London: Thin Man Press. Susan de Muth, translator.

Arendt, Hannah, 1962 [1951]. *The Origins of Totalitarianism*. New York: Meridian Books.

Arnett, Peter, 1968. "Major Describes Move." *New York Times*. February 8, 1968.

Associated Press, 2011. "Poll: Nearly 8 in 10 Americans Believe in Angels." *CBS News*. December 23, 2011. https://www.cbsnews.com/news/poll-nearly-8-in-10-americans-believe-in-angels/

Asturias, Miguel Angel, 1980 [1946]. *El Señor Presidente*. New York: Atheneum.

Bacevich, Andrew J., 2013. *The New American Militarism: How Americans Are Seduced by War*. Updated edition.. New York: Oxford University Press.

Bataille, Georges, 2006 [1994]. *The Absence of Myth: Writings on Surrealism*. London: Verso. Edited and translated by Michael Richardson.

Baudrillard, Jean, 2008. *The Perfect Crime*. London: Verso.

Beaujour, Michel, 1963. "Sartre and Surrealism." *Yale French Studies* (30): 86-95.

Belokowsky, Simon, 2019. "Laughing on the Inside: Humor as a Lens on Gulag Society." *Journal of Social History* **52** (4): 1281-1306.

Benjamin, Walter, 1978. "Surrealism: The Last Snapshot of the European Intelligentsia." *New Left Review* **I/108** (March-April 1978): 47-56.

Benjamin, Walter, 1999. *The Arcades Project*. Cambridge, MA: The Belknap Press of Harvard University Press.

Benjamin, Walter, 1999 [1935]. Paris, the Capital of the Nineteenth Century (Exposé of 1935). *The Arcades Project*. Cambridge: The Belknap Press of Harvard University Press.

Bernays, Edward, 2005 [1928]. *Propaganda*. Brooklyn, NY: IG Books.

Blomfield, Adrian, 2004. "How US Fuelled Myth of Zarqawi the Mastermind." *The Telegraph*. October 4, 2004. https://www.telegraph.co.uk/news/worldnews/middleeast/iraq/1473309/How-US-fuelled-myth-of-Zarqawi-the-mastermind.html

Blumenthal, Max, 2021. "Reuters, BBC, and Bellingcat

Participated in Covert UK Foreign Office-Funded Programs to "Weaken Russia," Leaked Docs Reveal." *The Grayzone.* February 20, 2021. https://thegrayzone.com/2021/02/20/ reuters-bbc-uk-foreign-office-russian-media/

Bly, Nellie, 2011 [1887]. *Ten Days in a Madhouse.* Milton Keynes: Amazon Marston Gate.

Bolduc, Nicholas S., 2016. "Global Insecurity: How Risk Theory Gave Rise to Global Police Militarization." *Indiana Journal of Global Legal Studies* **23** (1): 267-292.

Böll, Heinrich, 2010 [1979]. *The Safety Net.* New York: Melville House.

Borjesson, Kristina, 2004 [2002]. *Into the Buzzsaw: Leading Journalists Expose the Myth of the Free Press.* New York: Prometheus Books.

Breton, André, 2004 [1944]. *Arcanum 17.* Los Angeles: Green Integer. Zack Rogow, translator.

Breton, André, 2009 [1997]. *Anthology of Black Humour.* London: Telegram.

Breton, André, 2010 [1924]. Manifesto of Surrealism. *Manifestoes of Surrealism.* Ann Arbor: University of Michigan Press: 1-47.

Breton, André, 2010 [1930]. Second Manifesto of Surrealism. *Manifestoes of Surrealism.* Ann Arbor: University of Michigan Press.

Brown, Alleen and Akela Lacy, 2021. "State Legislatures Make

'Unprecedented' Push On Anti-Protest Bills." *The Intercept.* January 21, 2021. https://theintercept.com/2021/01/21/anti-protest-riot-state-laws/

Brown, Alleen, et al., 2017. "Leaked Documents Reveal Counterterrorism Tactics Used At Standing Rock To 'Defeat Pipeline Insurgencies'." *The Intercept.* May 27, 2017. https://theintercept.com/2017/05/27/leaked-documents-reveal-security-firms-counterterrorism-tactics-at-standing-rock-to-defeat-pipeline-insurgencies/

Buckley, Cara, 2007. "At least 9 killed in Baghdad attacks." *The New York Times.* November 10, 2007. https://www.nytimes.com/2007/12/10/world/africa/10iht-10iraq.3.8667855.html

Bush, George W., 2001. "President Bush Addresses the Nation [full text of his public address to a Joint Session of Congress]." *Washington Post.* September 20, 2001. http://www.washingtonpost.com/wp-srv/nation/specials/attacked/transcripts/bushaddress_092001.html

Carden, James, 2017. "The Chemical-Weapons Attack In Syria: Is There a Place for Skepticism?" *The Nation.* April 19, 2017. https://www.thenation.com/article/the-chemical-weapons-attack-in-syria-is-there-a-place-for-skepticism/

Carr, Adrian N. and Lisa A. Zanetti, 2000. "The Emergence of a Surrealist Movement and its Vital 'Estrangement-Effect' in Organization Studies." *Human Relations* **53** (7): 891-921.

Carrington, Leonora, 2005 [1974]. *The Hearing Trumpet.* New York: Penguin Books.
Carrington, Leonora, 2017 [1944]. *Down Below.* New York: New York Review of Books.

Carroll, Rory, 2013. "Welcome To Utah, The NSA's Desert Home For Eavesdropping On America." *The Guardian*. June 14, 2013. https://www.theguardian.com/world/2013/jun/14/nsa-utah-data-facility

Cartalucci, Tony, 2015. "TIME Admits ISIS Bringing Arms, Fighters in From NATO Territory." *New Eastern Outlook*. December 7, 2015. https://journal-neo.org/2015/07/12/time-admits-isis-bringing-arms-fighters-in-from-nato-territory/

Cave, Damien, 2007. "US identifies Qaeda official killed in Iraq." *The New York Times*. May 3, 2007. https://www.nytimes.com/2007/05/03/world/africa/03iht-iraq.4.5554349.html

Chabris, Christopher F. and Daniel J. Simons, 2010. *The invisible gorilla: and other ways our intuitions deceive us*. New York: Crown.

Chesterton, G.K., 2007 [1908]. *The Man Who Was Thursday*. London: Penguin Books.

Chomsky, Noam and Edward S. Herman, 2002 [1988]. *Manufacturing Consent*. New York: Pantheon Books.

Clair, Jean, 2001. "Surrealism and the demoralisation of the West." *Le Monde*. November 22, 2001.

Cobain, Ian, 2019. "Twitter Executive for Middle East Is British Army 'Psyops' Soldier" *Middle East Eye*. September 30, 2019. https://www.middleeasteye.net/news/twitter-executive-also-part-time-officer-uk-army-psychological-warfare-unit

Colman, Andrew M., 2009. *A Dictionary of Psychology*. Oxford University Press. https://www.oxfordreference.com/view/10.1093/acref/9780199534067.001.0001/

acref-9780199534067

Conrad, Joseph, 2015 [1907]. *The Secret Agent*. New Jersey: J.P. Piper Books.

Constantinidou, Despina-Alexandra, 2010. "The Paranoid Simulacrum in Surrealism: From Embracing Madness to the Mechanism of a Mental Illness as the Purveyor of Individual Meaning." *Gramma: Journal of Theory and Criticism* **18**: 119-133.

Crevel, René, 2004 [1933]. Notes Towards a Psycho-dialectic. *Surrealism*. Mary Ann Caws, ed. London: Phaidon: 265-267.

Cukor, George, 1944. *Gaslight*. Metro-Goldwyn-Mayer.

Dagher, Sam and Atheer Kakan, 2009. "Iraqi Premier Says Leader in Insurgency Is in Custody." *The New York Times*. April 28, 2009. https://www.nytimes.com/2009/04/29/world/middleeast/29iraq.html

Daley, Paul, 2020. "Julian Assange Indictment Fails To Mention Wikileaks Video That Exposed US 'War Crimes' In Iraq." *The Guardian*. June 14, 2020. https://www.theguardian.com/media/2020/jun/15/julian-assange-indictment-fails-to-mention-wikileaks-video-that-exposed-us-war-crimes-in-iraq

Dali, Salvador, 2004 [1930]. The Rotting Donkey. *Surrealism*. Mary Ann Caws, ed. London: Phaidon Press: 257-258.

David, Charter, 2017. "Thousands of CIA spy files posted on internet; British intelligence helped hack TVs and phones." *The Times (London)*. March 8, 2017. 1-2.

Davies, Nick, 2009. *Flat Earth News*. London: Vintage Books.

Davis, Tracy C., 2006. "Operation Northwoods: The Pentagon's Scripts for Overthrowing Castro." *TDR: The Drama Review* **50** (1): 134-148.

deHaven-Smith, Lance, 2013. *Conspiracy Theory in America*. Austin: University of Texas Press.

Deleuze, Gilles, 1992. "Postscript on the Societies of Control." *October* **59** (Winter): 3-7.

Deleuze, Gilles, 2001. "Philosophy of the *Série Noire*." *Genre* **34** (1-2): 5-10.

DeLillo, Don, 1991. *Mao II*. London: Penguin Books.

Diab, Robert, 2015. *The Harbinger Theory: How the Post-9/11 Emergency Became Permanent and the Case for Reform*. New York: Oxford University Press.

Douglass, William A. and Joseba Zulaika, 1996. *Terror and Taboo*. London: Routledge.

Duquette, Elizabeth, 2013. "Re-thinking American Exceptionalism." *Literature Compass* **10** (6): 473-482.

Dwoskin, Elizabeth, et al., 2016. "Why Facebook and Google Are Struggling to Purge Fake News." *The Washington Post*. November 15, 2016. https://www.washingtonpost.com/business/economy/why-facebook-and-google-are-struggling-to-purge-fake-news/2016/11/15/85022897-f765-422e-9f53-c720d1f20071_story.html

Eburne, Jonathan, 2003. Surrealism Noir. *Surrealism, Politics and Culture*. Donald LaCoss and Raymond Spiteri, ed. Aldershot: Ashgate.

Eburne, Jonathan, 2008. *Surrealism and the Art of Crime*. Ithaca: Cornell University Press.

Eburne, Jonathan P., 2005. "Object Lessons: Surrealist Art, Surrealist Politics." *Modernism/Modernity* **12** (1): 175-181.

Eco, Umberto, 1995. "Ur-Fascism." *New York Review of Books*. June 22, 1995.

Elmaazi, Mohamed and Max Blumenthal, 2018. "Inside the Temple of Covert Propaganda: The Integrity Initiative and the UK's Scandalous Information War." *The Grayzone*. December 17, 2018. https://thegrayzone.com/2018/12/17/inside-the-temple-of-covert-propaganda-the-integrity-initiative-and-the-uks-scandalous-information-war/

Erickson, John D., 1988. "Surrealist Black Humor as Oppositional Discourse." *Symposium: A Quarterly Journal in Modern Literatures* **42** (3): 198-215.

Erickson-Muschko, Sarah, 2013. "Beyond Individual Status: The Clear Statement Rule and the Scope of the AUMF Detention Authority in the United States." *Georgetown Law Journal* **101** (5): 1399-1649.

Fang, Lee, 2015. "Why was an FBI Joint Terrorism Task Force tracking a Black Lives Matter protest?" *The Intercept*. March 12, 2015. https://theintercept.com/2015/03/12/fbi-appeared-use-informant-track-black-lives-matter-protest/

Fang, Lee and Steve Horn, 2016. "Federal Agents Went Undercover To Spy on Anti-Fracking Movement, Emails Reveal." *The Intercept*. July 19, 2016. https://theintercept.com/2016/07/19/blm-fracking-protests/

Featherstone, Mark, 2000. "The obscure politics of conspiracy theory." *Sociological Review* **48** (S2): 31-45.

Filkins, Dexter, 2004. "US Says Files Seek Qaeda Aid In Iraq Conflict." *The New York Times*. February 9, 2004. https://www.nytimes.com/2004/02/09/world/the-struggle-for-iraq-intelligence-us-says-files-seek-qaeda-aid-in-iraq-conflict.html

Fisher, Mark, 2009. *Capitalist Realism: Is There No Alternative?* Winchester: Zero Books.

Fisk, Robert, 2015. "America siding with 'terrorists' like al-Nusra? It's not a conspiracy theory." *The Independent*. June 14, 2015. http://www.independent.co.uk/voices/comment/america-siding-with-terrorists-like-al-nusra-its-not-a-conspiracy-theory-10319370.html

Foucault, Michel, 2001. *The Order of Things*. London: Routledge.

Freedman, Des and Daya Kishan Thussu, 2012. *Media & Terrorism: Global Perspectives*. London: Sage Publications Ltd.

Friedersdorf, Conor, 2012. "How Team Obama Justifies the Killing of a 16-Year-Old American." *The Atlantic*. October 24, 2012. https://www.theatlantic.com/politics/archive/2012/10/how-team-obama-justifies-the-killing-of-a-16-year-old-american/264028/

Gabriel, Elliott, 2018. "Facebook Partners With Hawkish Atlantic Council, a NATO Lobby Group, to 'Protect Democracy'." *Mint Press News.* May 22, 2018. https://www.mintpressnews. com/facebook-partners-hawkish-atlantic-council-nato-lobby-group-protect-democracy/242289/

Ganguly, Sumit, 2015. *The Snowden Reader.* Bloomington: Indiana University Press. http://www.jstor.org/stable/j.ctt16gh840

Ganser, Daniele, 2004. *NATO's Secret Armies: Operation GLADIO and Terrorism in Western Europe.* New York: Routledge.

Gates, Robert, 2009. *Civil Action No. 08-cv-1360 (RWR): Respondent's Memorandum of Points and Authorities in Opposition to Petitioner's Motion for Discovery and Petitioner's Motion for Sanctions.* October 27, 2009. Washington, DC. United States District Court for the District of Columbia.

Gee, Harvey, 2015. "National Insecurity: The National Defense Authorization Act, the Indefinite Detention of American Citizens, and a Call for Heightened Judicial Scrutiny." *John Marshall Law Review* **49** (1): 69-100.

Georgeanne A, Wallen, 2014. "Becoming an Orwellian Society: Big Brother Is Watching You." *Thurgood Marshall Law Review* **40** (1): 65-77.

Giglio, Mike, 2020. "A Pro-Trump Militant Group Has Recruited Thousands of Police, Soldiers, and Veterans." *The Atlantic.* https://www.theatlantic.com/magazine/archive/2020/11/right-wing-militias-civil-war/616473/

Gordon, Michael R., 2002. "A Nation Challenged: Bin Laden Lieutenant; A Top Qaeda Commander Believed Seized in

Pakistan." *The New York Times*. March 30, 2002. p 12.

Gordon, Michael R., 2007. "Leader of Al Qaeda group in Iraq was fictional, US military says." *The New York Times*. July 18, 2007. http://www.nytimes.com/2007/07/18/world/africa/18iht-iraq.4.6718200.html

Graff, Vincent, 2004. "Meet the Yes Men Who Hoax the World." *The Guardian*. December 13, 2004. https://www.theguardian.com/media/2004/dec/13/mondaymediasection5

Greenwald, Glenn, 2013. "The Crux Of The NSA Story In One Phrase: 'Collect It All'." *The Guardian*. July 15, 2013. https://www.theguardian.com/commentisfree/2013/jul/15/crux-nsa-collect-it-all

Greenwald, Glenn, 2020. "Facebook and Twitter Cross a Line Far More Dangerous Than What They Censor." *The Intercept*. October 16, 2020. https://theintercept.com/2020/10/15/facebook-and-twitter-cross-a-line-far-more-dangerous-than-what-they-censor/

Greenwald, Glenn and Andrew Fishman, 2015a. "Controversial GCHQ Unit Engaged In Domestic Law Enforcement, Online Propaganda, Psychology Research." *The Intercept*. June 22, 2015. https://theintercept.com/2015/06/22/controversial-gchq-unit-domestic-law-enforcement-propaganda/

Greenwald, Glenn and Andrew Fishman, 2015b. "Latest FBI Claim of Disrupted Terror Plot Deserves Much Scrutiny and Skepticism." *The Intercept*. January 16, 2015. https://theintercept.com/2015/01/16/latest-fbi-boast-disrupting-terror-u-s-plot-deserves-scrutiny-skepticism/

Hargrove, Thomas, 2006. *Third of Americans Suspect 9/11 Government Conspiracy*. Scripps Howard/Ohio University Poll. Cincinatti: Scripps Howard News Service. August 1, 2006. https://web.archive.org/web/20060805052538/http://www.scrippsnews.com/911poll

Haynes, Doug, 2006. "The Persistence of Irony: Interfering with Surrealist Black Humour." *Textual Practice* **20** (1): 25-47.

Heilbrunn, Jacob, 2011. "Inside the world of conspiracy theorists." *The New York Times*. May 13, 2011. http://www.nytimes.com/2011/05/15/books/review/book-review-among-the-truthers-by-jonathan-kay.html?_r=0

Henderson, Ian, 2020. Reply to Your Letter of Censure. OPCW Director-General. https://thegrayzone.com/wp-content/uploads/2020/03/Inspector-A-Letter-to-DG.pdf

Hendricks, Jon and Jean Toche, 1978. *GAAG: The Guerrilla Art Action Group*. New York: Printed Matter, Inc.

Hertz, Erich, 2010. "Disruptive Testimonies: The Stakes of Surrealist Experience in Breton and Carrington." *Symposium* **64** (2): 15.

Higgins, Elliot, 2019. Consecutive tweets. https://twitter.com/EliotHiggins/status/1129398851725664256

Hirsch, Afua, 2009. "Police Accused Of Misusing Terror Laws Against Peaceful Protests." *The Guardian*. March 23, 2009. https://www.theguardian.com/uk/2009/mar/23/police-terrorism-protest-g20-law

History Commons, undated-a. "Profile: Ali Mohamed." Retrieved

March 23, 2021, from http://www.historycommons.org/entity.jsp?entity=ali_mohamed.

History Commons, undated-b. "Profile: Anwar Al-Awlaki." Retrieved March 25, 2021, from http://www.historycommons.org/entity.jsp?entity=anwar_al_aulaqi.

Hitchens, Peter, 2020. "Justice Denied: How Authority Tried to Ignore and then Bury Honest Dissent by Responsible Scientists." *The Daily Mail*. February 29, 2020. https://hitchensblog.mailonsunday.co.uk/2020/02/a-and-b-respond-to-the-opcws-attacks-on-them-the-full-rebuttal.html

Hofstadter, Richard, 1964. "The Paranoid Style in American Politics." *Harper's*. November 1964. 77-86.

Horkheimer, Max and Theodor W. Adorno, 2002 [1944]. *Dialectic of Enlightenment*. Stanford: Stanford University Press. Edmund Jephcott, translator.

Human Rights Watch, 2014a. *Illusion of Justice: Human Rights Abuses in US Terrorism Prosecutions*. Human Rights Watch. July 21, 2014. https://www.hrw.org/report/2014/07/21/illusion-justice/human-rights-abuses-us-terrorism-prosecutions

Human Rights Watch, 2014b. *US Terrorism Prosecutions Often an Illusion*. July 21, 2014. https://www.hrw.org/news/2014/07/21/us-terrorism-prosecutions-often-illusion

Hunt, Jamer, 1999. Paranoid, Critical, Methodical, Dali, Koolhaas, and... *Paranoia Within Reason: A Casebook on Conspiracy as Explanation*. George E. Marcus, ed. Chicago: University of Chicago Press.

James, Klem, 2009. "Breton, Bataille and Lacan's Notion of "Transgressive" Sublimation." *E-pisteme* **2** (1): 53-66.

Jamieson, Kathleen Hall and Paul Waldman, 2003. *The Press Effect: Politicians, Journalists, and the Stories that Shape the Political World*. Oxford: Oxford University Press.

Kay, Jonathan, 2011. *Among the Truthers: A Journey Through America's Growing Conspiracist Underground*. New York: Harper.

Kean, Thomas and Lee Hamilton, 2004. *The 9/11 Commission Report: Final Report of the National Commission on Terrorist Attacks Upon the United States*. Authorized ed. New York: W. W. Norton.

Kutz-Flamenbaum, Rachel V., 2014. "Humor and Social Movements." *Sociology Compass* **8** (3): 294-304.

Lacan, Jacques, 1933. "Motives of Paranoiac Crime: The Crime of the Papin Sisters." Originally published in *Minotaure* 3-4, December 1933. http://www.lacan.com/papin.htm.

LaCoss, Donald, 2003. Attacks of the Fantastic. *Surrealism, Politics, and Culture*. Donald LaCoss and Raymond Spiteri, ed. Aldershot: Ashgate.

LaCoss, Donald and Raymond Spiteri, 2003. *Surrealism, Politics and Culture*. Aldershot: Ashgate.

Lauria, Joe, 2021. "There Were No Calls for Censorship Against Democrats for Their False Claims About the 2016 Election." *Consortium News*. March 1, 2021. https://consortiumnews. com/2021/03/01/there-were-no-calls-for-censorship-against-democrats-for-their-false-claims-about-the-2016-

election/

Leng, Kirsten, 2020. "Art, Humor, and Activism: The Sardonic, Sustaining Feminism of the Guerrilla Girls, 1985–2000." *Journal of Women's History* **32** (4): 110-134.

Lethem, Jonathan, 2012. *Talking Heads' Fear of Music*. New York: Continuum.

Lethem, Jonathan, 2015. Skype Call with Jonathan Lethem. August 22, 2015. Interviewed by John Schoneboom.

Levin, Sam, 2017. "Revealed: FBI terrorism taskforce investigating Standing Rock activists." *The Guardian*. February 10, 2017. https://www.theguardian.com/us-news/2017/feb/10/standing-rock-fbi-investigation-dakota-access

Levin, Sam, 2019. "Revealed: FBI Investigated Civil Rights Group As 'Terrorism' Threat And Viewed KKK As Victims." *The Guardian*. February 1, 2019. https://www.theguardian.com/us-news/2019/feb/01/sacramento-rally-fbi-kkk-domestic-terrorism-california

Levy, Rachael, 2021. "Biden Administration Urged to Take Fresh Look at Domestic Terrorism." *The Wall Street Journal*. November 13, 2020. https://archive.is/IrqNp

Lewis, Paul, 2014. "Obama Admits CIA 'Tortured Some Folks' But Stands By Brennan Over Spyinga." *The Guardian*. August 1, 2014. https://www.theguardian.com/world/2014/aug/01/obama-cia-torture-some-folks-brennan-spying

Licklider, Roy, 1970. "The missile gap controversy." *Political*

Science Quarterly **85** (4): 600-615.

Lindström, Per, 1997. "Persuasion via facts in political discussion." *European Journal of Social Psychology* **27** (2): 145-163.

Lippmann, Walter, 2010 [1920]. *Liberty and the News*. New York: Dover Publications, Inc.

Lotto, Beau, 2018. *Deviate: The Creative Power of Transforming Your Perception*. 2nd. London: Wiedenfeld & Nicolson.

Marcus, George E., Ed. 1999. *Paranoia Within Reason: A Casebook on Conspiracy as Explanation*. Late Editions: Cultural Studies for the End of the Century. Chicago, University of Chicago Press.

Marcuse, Herbert, 1991 [1964]. *One-Dimensional Man: Studies in the Ideology of Advanced Industrial Society*. Boston: Beacon Press.

Marr, Andrew, 1996. "Interview with Noam Chomsky." *The Big Idea (BBC)*. February 1996. https://www.youtube.com/watch?v=GjENnyQupow&t=557s

Martin, Gerald, 1989. *Journeys through the Labyrinth: Latin American Fiction in the Twentieth Century*. London: Verso.

Mate, Aaron, 2020a. "Did Trump Bomb Syria on False Grounds?" *The Nation*. July 24, 2020. https://www.thenation.com/article/world/opcw-leaks-syria/

Mate, Aaron, 2020b. "Draft Debacle: Bellingcat Smears OPCW Whistleblower, Journalists with False Letter,

Farcical Claims." *The Grayzone*. October 28, 2020. https://thegrayzone.com/2020/10/28/draft-debacle-bellingcat-smears-opcw-whistleblower-journalists-with-false-letter-farcical-claims/

Mate, Aaron, 2020c. "Exclusive: OPCW Chief Made False Claims to Denigrate Douma Whistleblower, Documents Reveal." *The Grayzone*. May 6, 2020. https://thegrayzone.com/2020/05/06/opcw-douma-whistleblower/

Mate, Aaron, 2020d. "OPCW Syria Whistleblower and Ex-Director Attacked by US, UK, France at UN." *The Grayzone*. October 7, 2020. https://thegrayzone.com/2020/10/07/opcw-syria-whistleblower-and-ex-opcw-chief-attacked-by-us-uk-french-at-un/

McKeigue, Paul, et al., 2018. *Briefing Note on the Integrity Initiative*. Propaganda and Media Working Group on syria. https://syriapropagandamedia.org/working-papers/briefing-note-on-the-integrity-initiative

Mekhennet, Souad, 2014. "The terrorists fighting us now? We just finished training them." *The Washington Post*. August 18, 2014. https://www.washingtonpost.com/posteverything/wp/2014/08/18/the-terrorists-fighting-us-now-we-just-finished-training-them/?utm_term=.93fe74355311

Mickey, Thomas J., 1997. "A postmodern view of public relations: Sign and reality." *Public Relations Review* **23** (3): 271-284.

Miller, Kevin, 2014. "Total surveillance, big data, and predictive crime technology: privacy's perfect storm." *Journal of Technology Law & Policy* **19** (1): 41.

Milne, Seumas, 2015. "Now the Truth Emerges: How the

US Fuelled the Rise of ISIS in Syria and Iraq." *The Guardian*. June 3, 2015. https://www.theguardian.com/commentisfree/2015/jun/03/us-isis-syria-iraq

Moïse, Edwin E., 1996. *Tonkin Gulf and the Escalation of the Vietnam War*. Chapel Hill: University of North Carolina Press.

Monahan, Laurie J., 2001. "Violence in Paradise: Andre Masson's 'Massacres'." *Art History* **24** (5): 707.

Morris, Nigel, 2015. "Edward Snowden: GCHQ Collected Information From Every Visible User On The Internet." *The Independent*. September 25, 2015. https://www.independent.co.uk/news/uk/home-news/edward-snowden-gchq-collected-information-every-visible-user-internet-10517356.html

Mortimer, Caroline, 2015. "What turns someone into a conspiracy theorist? Study to look at why some are more 'receptive' to such theories." *The Independent*. July 30, 2015. http://www.independent.co.uk/news/uk/home-news/what-turns-someone-into-a-conspiracy-theorist-study-to-look-at-why-some-are-more-receptive-to-such-10427940.html

Murray, Nancy, 2011. "Obama and the global war on terror." *Race & Class* **53** (2): 9.

Myers, Steven Lee, 2010. "Iraqi Insurgent Group Acknowledges Killing of Two Leaders." *The New York Times*. April 25, 2010. https://www.nytimes.com/2010/04/26/world/middleeast/26iraq.html

Nathanson, Rebecca, 2021. "Terrorism-Related Convictions

Overturned For UK Activists Who Blocked Deportations."
The Intercept. January 29, 2021. https://theintercept.
com/2021/01/29/stansted-15-terrorism-deportation-
overturn/

Nietzsche, Friedrich Wilhelm, 2000 [1872]. *The Birth of Tragedy.*
Oxford: Oxford University Press.

Norden, Eric, 1967. "Interview with Jim Garrison." *Playboy.*
October 1967.

Norton, Ben, 2020. "OPCW Investigator Testifies at UN that No
Chemical Attack Took Place in Douma, Syria." *The Grayzone.*
January 22, 2020. https://thegrayzone.com/2020/01/22/ian-
henderson-opcw-whistleblower-un-no-chemical-attack-
douma-syria/

Norton, Ben and Glenn Greenwald, 2016. "Washington Post
Disgracefully Promotes a McCarthyite Blacklist From
a New, Hidden, and Very Shady Group." *The Intercept.*
November 26, 2016. https://theintercept.com/2016/11/26/
washington-post-disgracefully-promotes-a-mccarthyite-
blacklist-from-a-new-hidden-and-very-shady-group/

Norton-Taylor, Richard, 2015. "Terror Trial Collapses after
Fears of Deep Embarrassment to Security Services." *The
Guardian.* June 1, 2015. https://www.theguardian.com/uk-
news/2015/jun/01/trial-swedish-man-accused-terrorism-
offences-collapse-bherlin-gildo

Oaklander, Mandy, 2015. "Here's why people believe in
conspiracy theories." *Time.* August 14, 2015. http://time.
com/3997033/conspiracy-theories/

Obadare, Ebenezer, 2009. "The Uses of Ridicule: Humour,

'Infrapolitics' and Civil Society in Nigeria." *African Affairs* **108** (431): 241-261.

Olesen, Thomas, 2007. "The Funny Side of Globalization: Humour and Humanity in Zapatista Framing." *International Review of Social History* **52** (S15): 21-34.

OPCW, 2019. *Report of the OPCW Fact-Finding Mission in Syria Regarding the Incident of Alleged Use of Toxic Chemicals as a Weapon in Douma, Syrian Arab Republic, On 7 April 2018.* Organization for the Prohibition of Chemical Weapons. https://www.opcw.org/sites/default/files/documents/2019/03/s-1731-2019%28e%29.pdf

OPCW, 2020. *Director-General's Statement on the Report of the Investigation into Possible Breaches of Confidentiality.* February 6, 2020. https://www.opcw.org/sites/default/files/documents/2020/02/OPCW%20Director-General's%20Statement%20on%20the%20Report%20of%20the%20Investigation%20into%20Possible%20Breaches%20of%20Confidentiality.pdf

OPCW Fact-Finding Mission, 2019. Engineering Assessment of Two Cylinders Observed at the Douma Incident (leaked document). https://drive.google.com/file/d/1ayBv-nEOMTtIc-QOvejQBdCnZQXTuJ5z/view

Orwell, George, 1968. Funny But Not Vulgar. *The Collected Essays, Journalism and Letters of George Orwell, Vol. 3 As I Please, 1943–1945.* Sonia Orwell and Ian Angus, ed. New York: Harcourt Brace Jovanovitch.

Palast, Greg, 2014. "Jim Crow Returns." *Al Jazeera.* October 29, 2014. http://projects.aljazeera.com/2014/double-voters/

index.html

Pamatmat, Matthew, California State University, 2007. Hyper-Surrealism: A Successor to Postmodernism. *Humanities.* Dominguez Hills, California State University. MA.

Parry, Robert, 2015. "The Mess that Nuland Made." *Consortium News.* July 13, 2015. https://consortiumnews.com/2015/07/13/the-mess-that-nuland-made/

Paye, Jean-Claude, 2006. "A Permanent State of Emergency." *Monthly Review* **58** (5): 29.

Ponsonby, Arthur, 2005 [1928]. *Falsehood in War Time: Containing an Assortment of Lies Circulated throughout the Nations during the Great War.* Whitefish, MT: Kessinger Publishing.

Porter, Gareth, 2016. *Reporting (or Not) the Ties Between US-Armed Syrian Rebels and Al Qaeda's Affiliate.* Fairness and Accuracy In Reporting (FAIR). March 21, 2016. http://fair.org/home/reporting-or-not-the-ties-between-us-armed-syrian-rebels-and-al-qaedas-affiliate/

Powell, Jefferson, 2016. *Targeting Americans: The Constitutionality of the US Drone War.* New York: Oxford University Press.

PropOrNot, 2016. "The List." Retrieved March 2, 2021, from http://www.propornot.com/p/the-list.html.

Proulx, Travis, et al., 2010. "When Is the Unfamiliar the Uncanny? Meaning Affirmation After Exposure to Absurdist Literature, Humor, and Art." *Personality and Social Psychology Bulletin* **36** (6): 817-829.

Richardson, Michael and Krzysztof Fijalkowski, 2001. *Surrealism Against the Current: Tracts and Declarations*. London: Pluto Press.

Ricks, Thomas E., 2006. "Military Plays Up Role of Zarqawi." *The Washington Post*. April 10, 2006. https://www. washingtonpost.com/wp-dyn/content/article/2006/04/09/ AR2006040900890.html

Ristić, Marko, 2015 [1933]. Humour as a Moral Attitude. *The Surrealism Reader: An Anthology of Ideas*. Dawn Ades and Michael Richardson, ed. London: Tate Publishing.

Ritter, Scott, 2005. *Iraq Confidential: The Untold Story of America's Intelligence Conspiracy*. London: I.B.Tauris.

Romm, Tony, et al., 2020. "Facebook, Google, Twitter CEOs Clash with Congress in Pre-Election Showdown." *The Washington Post*. October 28, 2020. https://www.washingtonpost.com/ technology/2020/10/28/twitter-facebook-google-senate-hearing-live-updates/

Rosemont, Franklin, 1989a. *Arsenal: Surrealist Subversion, No. 4*. Chicago: Black Swan Press.

Rosemont, Franklin, 1989b. Humor: Here Today and Everywhere Tomorrow. *Arsenal/Surrealist Subversion*. Chicago: Black Swan Press.

Rosemont, Franklin, 2008. *Jacques Vaché and the Roots of Surrealism*. Chicago: Charles H. Kerr Publishing Co.

Rosenberg, Pnina, 2002. "Mickey Mouse in Gurs – humour, irony and criticism in works of art produced in the Gurs internment camp." *Rethinking history* **6** (3): 273-292.

Rosenhan, D. L., 1973. "On Being Sane in Insane Places." *Science* **179** (4070): 250-258.

Rowse, Arthur E., 1992. "How to build support for a war. (Public relations and the Persian Gulf War)." *Columbia Journalism Review* **31** (3): 28.

Rubinstein, Alexander, 2021. "CIA Pressured Yemen to Release Al Qaeda Leader from Prison." *Mint Press News*. March 23, 2021. https://www.mintpressnews.com/ leaked-cia-pressured-yemen-release-al-qaeda-anwar-al-awlaki/276327/

Ryan, Kevin, 2012. "Abu Zubaydah Poses a Real Threat to Al Qaeda." October 15, 2012. Retrieved May 11, 2017, from https://digwithin.net/2012/10/15/zubaydah/.

Sack, Kevin, 2017. "Door-Busting Drug Raids Leave a Trail of Blood." *The New York Times*. March 18, 2017. https:// www.nytimes.com/interactive/2017/03/18/us/forced-entry-warrant-drug-raid.html?_r=0

Sadowski, Jathan, 2013. "Ron Wyden's Warning: America May Be on Track to Become Surveillance State." *Slate*. July 23, 2013. https://slate.com/technology/2013/07/ron-wyden-dangers-of-nsa-surveillance-and-the-patriot-act.html

San Juan Jr., Epifanio, 2004. *Working Through the Contradictions: From Cultural Theory to Critical Practice*. Lewisburg: Bucknell University Press.

Sanders, Rebecca, 2011. "(Im)plausible legality: the

rationalisation of human rights abuses in the American 'Global War on Terror'." *The International Journal of Human Rights* **15** (4): 605-626.

Sanger, David E., 2012. "Rebel Arms Flow Is Said to Benefit Jihadists in Syria." *The New York Times*. October 14, 2012. http://www.nytimes.com/2012/10/15/world/middleeast/jihadists-receiving-most-arms-sent-to-syrian-rebels.html

Savage, Charlie, 2011. "Senators Say Patriot Act Is Being Misinterpreted." *The New York Times*. May 26, 2011. https://www.nytimes.com/2011/05/27/us/27patriot.html

Savage, Luke, 2021. "We Should Be Very Worried About Joe Biden's 'Domestic Terrorism' Bill." *Jacobin Magazine*. January 12, 2021. https://www.jacobinmag.com/2021/01/joe-biden-domestic-terrorism-bill-capitol-building

Scanlan, Margaret, 2001. *Plotting Terror*. Charlottesville: The University Press of Virginia.

Schaefer, Diane, 2002. "Police gang intelligence infiltrates a small city." *The Social Science Journal* **39** (1): 95-107.

Semple, Kirk, 2007. "Suicide Car Bomber Kills 7 Soldiers in Baghdad." *The New York Times*. March 10, 2007. https://www.nytimes.com/2007/03/10/world/middleeast/10cnd-baghdad.html

Shipler, David, 2012. "Terrorist Plots, Hatched by the FBI." *The New York Times*. April 28, 2012. http://www.nytimes.com/2012/04/29/opinion/sunday/terrorist-plots-helped-along-by-the-fbi.html

Short, Robert, 2003. The Politics of Surrealism, 1920-1936.

Surrealism, Politics, and Culture. Donald LaCoss and Raymond Spiteri, ed. Aldershot: Ashgate.

Sick, Gary, 1991. *October Surprise: America's Hostages in Iran and the Election of Ronald Reagan.* New York: Random House.

Simons, Barbara and Eugene H. Spafford, 2003. "Risks of Total Surveillance." *Communications of the ACM* **46** (3): 120-120.

Slackman, Michael and Souad Mekhennet, 2008. "Jihadi Leader Says Radicals Share Obama Victory." *The New York Times.* November 7, 2008. https://www.nytimes.com/2008/11/08/world/middleeast/08jihadi.html

Snyders, Matt, 2008. "Whack a Mole." *City Pages.* June 3, 2008. http://blogs.citypages.com/blotter/2008/06/whackamole.php

Spinney, Franklin, 2011. "The Domestic Roots of Perpetual War." *Challenge* **54** (1): 15.

Stanford, Ben, 2015. "The 'War on Terror': Perpetual Emergency." *Edinburgh Student Law Review* **2** (4): 16.

Steele, Jonathan, 2019. "The OPCW and Douma: Chemical Weapons Watchdog Accused of Evidence-Tampering by Its Own Inspectors." *Counterpunch.* November 15, 2019. https://www.counterpunch.org/2019/11/15/the-opcw-and-douma-chemical-weapons-watchdog-accused-of-evidence-tampering-by-its-own-inspectors/

Street, Sarah, 2009. *British National Cinema.* London: Routledge.

Sunstein, Cass R. and Adrian Vermeule, 2008. "Conspiracy

Theories: Causes and Cures." *The Journal of Political Philosophy* **17** (2): 202-227.

Swift, Art, 2013. "Gallup Poll: Majority in US Still Believe JFK Killed in a Conspiracy." Retrieved April 28, 2017, from http://www.gallup.com/poll/165893/majority-believe-jfk-killed-conspiracy.aspx.

Swift, Art, 2017. "In US, Belief in Creationist View of Humans at New Low (38%)." Retrieved April 28, 2017, from http://www.gallup.com/poll/210956/belief-creationist-view-humans-new-low.aspx

Sylvain, Olivier, 2014. "Failing expectations: Fourth Amendment doctrine in the era of total surveillance." *Wake Forest Law Review* **49** (2): 38.

Taibbi, Matt, 2020. "The YouTube Ban Is Un-American, Wrong, and Will Backfire." *Substack*. https://taibbi.substack.com/p/the-youtube-ban-is-un-american-wrong

Taussig, Michael, 1984. "Culture of Terror/Space of Death." *Comparative Studies in Society and History* **26** (3): 467-497.

Taussig, Michael, 1987. *Shamanism, Colonialism, and the Wild Man*. Chicago: University of Chicago Press.

Taussig, Michael, 2008. "Zoology, Magic, and Surrealism in the War on Terror." *Critical Enquiry* **34** (S2): S98-S116.

Taylor, G. Flint, 2014. "The FBI COINTELPRO Program and the Fred Hampton Assassination." *The Huffington Post*. February 2, 2014. https://www.huffpost.com/entry/the-fbi-cointelpro-progra_b_4375527

The Nation, 2010. "Slide Show: Were The Newburgh Four Victims of FBI Entrapment?" *The Nation*. November 12, 2010. https://www.thenation.com/article/archive/slide-show-were-newburgh-four-victims-fbi-entrapment/

Timm, Trevor, 2011. *Ten Years After the Patriot Act, a Look at Three of the Most Dangerous Provisions Affecting Ordinary Americans*. Electronic Frontier Foundation. October 26, 2011. https://www.eff.org/deeplinks/2011/10/ten-years-later-look-three-scariest-provisions-usa-patriot-act

Twitter Safety, 2021. Disclosing Networks of State-Linked Information Operations. https://blog.twitter.com/en_us/topics/company/2021/disclosing-networks-of-state-linked-information-operations-.html

US Senate, 1995. *S.390 Omnibus Counterterrorism Act of 1995*. https://www.congress.gov/bill/104th-congress/senate-bill/390

US Senate, 2001. *Congressional Record, Volume 147, Number 144*. https://www.govinfo.gov/content/pkg/CREC-2001-10-25/html/CREC-2001-10-25-pt1-PgS10990-2.htm

Valentine, Douglas, 2017. *The CIA as Organized Crime*. Atlanta: Clarity Press.

Van Natta Jr., Don, 2006. "Bush Was Set on Path to War, British Memo Says." *The New York Times*. March 27, 2006. http://www.nytimes.com/2006/03/27/world/europe/bush-was-set-on-path-towar-british-memo-says.html

Vaneigem, Raoul, 1999 [1977]. *A Cavalier History of Surrealism*. Edinburgh: AK Press. Donald Nicholson-Smith, translator.

Vian, Boris, 2011 [1948]. *To Hell with the Ugly*. Los Angeles: TamTam Books. Paul Knobloch, translator.

Vidal, John and Helen Pidd, 2007. "Police To Use Terror Laws On Heathrow Climate Protesters." *The Guardian*. August 11, 2007. https://www.theguardian.com/uk/2007/aug/11/ukcrime.greenpolitics

Vries, Lloyd, 2002. "Hijackers Lived with FBI Informant." *CBS News*. September 9, 2002. https://www.cbsnews.com/news/hijackers-lived-with-fbi-informant/

Wala, Michael, 2016. "Stay-behind operations, former members of SS and Wehrmacht, and American intelligence services in early Cold War Germany." *Journal of Intelligence History* **15** (2): 71-79.

Walsh, Declan, 2010. "WikiLeaks Cables Portray Saudi Arabia as a Cash Machine for Terrorists." *The Guardian*. December 5, 2010. https://www.theguardian.com/world/2010/dec/05/wikileaks-cables-saudi-terrorist-funding

Warzel, Charlie, 2021. "Don't Go Down the Rabbit Hole." *The New York Times*. February 18, 2021. https://www.nytimes.com/2021/02/18/opinion/fake-news-media-attention.html?

Westerhoff, Jan, 2010. *Twelve Examples of Illusion*. Oxford: Oxford University Press.

White, Hayden V., 1985 [1978]. *Tropics of Discourse: Essays in Cultural Criticism*. Baltimore: Johns Hopkins University Press.

Whitehead, John W., 2013. *A Government of Wolves: The Emerging*

American Police State. New York: Select Books Inc.

Wikileaks, 2019. "OPCW-Douma Docs." Retrieved February 18, 2021, from https://wikileaks.org/opcw-douma/releases/#OPCW%20Whistleblower%20Panel%20on%20the%20Douma%20attack%20of%20April%202018.

Wikipedia. "Martha Mitchell Effect." Retrieved March 15, 2021, from https://en.wikipedia.org/wiki/Martha_Mitchell_effect.

Wintour, Patrick and Bethan McKernan, 2020. "Inquiry Strikes Blow to Russian Denials of Syria Chemical Attack." *The Guardian.* February 7, 2020. https://www.theguardian.com/world/2020/feb/07/inquiry-strikes-blow-to-russian-denials-of-syria-chemical-attack

Wolf, Naomi, 2007. *The End of America: Letter of Warning to a Young Patriot.* White River Junction, VT: Chelsea Green Publishing.

Wolf, Naomi, 2012. "Revealed: How the FBI Coordinated the Crackdown on Occupy." *The Guardian.* December 29, 2012. https://www.theguardian.com/commentisfree/2012/dec/29/fbi-coordinated-crackdown-occupy

Wolin, Sheldon, 2010 [2008]. *Democracy Inc.* Princeton: Princeton University Press.

Žižek, Slavoj, 2006. *How to Read Lacan.* Kindle Edition. London: Granta.

Zogby International, 2004, August 30, 2004. "Half of New Yorkers Believe US Leaders Had Foreknowledge of Impending 9-11

Attacks and 'Consciously Failed' To Act." Retrieved June 4, 2016, from https://web.archive.org/web/20081217161036/ http://www.zogby.com/search/ReadNews.dbm?ID=855.

Author Biography

John Schoneboom is the author of the novel *Fontoon* (Dedalus Books) and a number of plays produced for Off-Off Broadway venues. He is the founding editor of Bratum Books' *Uncommonalities* series of short stories that share a common first line, to which he also shamelessly contributes his own efforts. His word-collage play *Dreams of Jimmy Bannon* won the Artists' Fellowship Award from the Massachusetts Cultural Council, and an extract from a novel under development won a Northern Writers' Award from New Writing North, supported in part by Arts Council England. His PhD (Northumbria University) was on the terrorism novel in a surrealist mode, and he also holds MAs in creative writing (Northumbria) and science, technology, and international affairs (George Washington University) and a BA focusing on US foreign policy in Central America (Hampshire College). Originally from New York, Schoneboom now resides in Newcastle upon Tyne.

CULTURE, SOCIETY & POLITICS

Contemporary culture has eliminated the concept and public figure of the intellectual. A cretinous anti-intellectualism presides, cheer-led by hacks in the pay of multinational corporations who reassure their bored readers that there is no need to rouse themselves from their stupor. Zer0 Books knows that another kind of discourse - intellectual without being academic, popular without being populist - is not only possible: it is already flourishing. Zer0 is convinced that in the unthinking, blandly consensual culture in which we live, critical and engaged theoretical reflection is more important than ever before.

If you have enjoyed this book, why not tell other readers by posting a review on your preferred book site.

You may also wish to
subscribe to our Zer0 Books YouTube Channel.

Bestsellers from Zer0 Books include:

Give Them An Argument
Logic for the Left
Ben Burgis
Many serious leftists have learned to distrust talk of logic. This is
a serious mistake.
Paperback: 978-1-78904-210-8 ebook: 978-1-78904-211-5

Poor but Sexy
Culture Clashes in Europe East and West
Agata Pyzik
How the East stayed East and the West stayed West.
Paperback: 978-1-78099-394-2 ebook: 978-1-78099-395-9

An Anthropology of Nothing in Particular
Martin Demant Frederiksen
A journey into the social lives of meaninglessness.
Paperback: 978-1-78535-699-5 ebook: 978-1-78535-700-8

In the Dust of This Planet
Horror of Philosophy vol. 1
Eugene Thacker
In the first of a series of three books on the Horror of Philosophy,
In the Dust of This Planet offers the genre of horror as a way of
thinking about the unthinkable.
Paperback: 978-1-84694-676-9 ebook: 978-1-78099-010-1

The End of Oulipo?
An Attempt to Exhaust a Movement
Lauren Elkin, Veronica Esposito
Paperback: 978-1-78099-655-4 ebook: 978-1-78099-656-1

Capitalist Realism
Is There No Alternative?
Mark Fisher
An analysis of the ways in which capitalism has presented itself
as the only realistic political-economic system.
Paperback: 978-1-84694-317-1 ebook: 978-1-78099-734-6

Rebel Rebel
Chris O'Leary
David Bowie: every single song. Everything you want to know,
everything you didn't know.
Paperback: 978-1-78099-244-0 ebook: 978-1-78099-713-1

Kill All Normies
Angela Nagle
Online culture wars from 4chan and Tumblr to Trump.
Paperback: 978-1-78535-543-1 ebook: 978-1-78535-544-8

Cartographies of the Absolute
Alberto Toscano, Jeff Kinkle
An aesthetics of the economy for the twenty-first century.
Paperback: 978-1-78099-275-4 ebook: 978-1-78279-973-3

Malign Velocities
Accelerationism and Capitalism
Benjamin Noys
Long listed for the Bread and Roses Prize 2015, *Malign Velocities*
argues against the need for speed, tracking acceleration
as the symptom of the ongoing crises of capitalism.
Paperback: 978-1-78279-300-7 ebook: 978-1-78279-299-4

Meat Market
Female Flesh under Capitalism
Laurie Penny
A feminist dissection of women's bodies as the fleshy fulcrum of capitalist cannibalism, whereby women are both consumers and consumed.
Paperback: 978-1-84694-521-2 ebook: 978-1-84694-782-7

Babbling Corpse
Vaporwave and the Commodification of Ghosts
Grafton Tanner
Paperback: 978-1-78279-759-3 ebook: 978-1-78279-760-9

New Work New Culture
Work we want and a culture that strengthens us
Frithjof Bergmann
A serious alternative for mankind and the planet.
Paperback: 978-1-78904-064-7 ebook: 978-1-78904-065-4

Romeo and Juliet in Palestine
Teaching Under Occupation
Tom Sperlinger
Life in the West Bank, the nature of pedagogy and the role of a university under occupation.
Paperback: 978-1-78279-637-4 ebook: 978-1-78279-636-7

Color, Facture, Art and Design
Iona Singh
This materialist definition of fine-art develops guidelines for architecture, design, cultural-studies and ultimately social change.
Paperback: 978-1-78099-629-5 ebook: 978-1-78099-630-1

Neglected or Misunderstood
The Radical Feminism of Shulamith Firestone
Victoria Margree
An interrogation of issues surrounding gender, biology,
sexuality, work and technology, and the ways in which our
imaginations continue to be in thrall to ideologies of maternity
and the nuclear family.
Paperback: 978-1-78535-539-4 ebook: 978-1-78535-540-0

How to Dismantle the NHS in 10 Easy Steps (Second Edition)
Youssef El-Gingihy
The story of how your NHS was sold off and why you will have
to buy private health insurance soon. A new expanded second
edition with chapters on junior doctors' strikes and government
blueprints for US-style healthcare.
Paperback: 978-1-78904-178-1 ebook: 978-1-78904-179-8

Digesting Recipes
The Art of Culinary Notation
Susannah Worth
A recipe is an instruction, the imperative tone of the expert, but
this constraint can offer its own kind of potential. A recipe need
not be a domestic trap but might instead offer escape – something
to fantasise about or aspire to.
Paperback: 978-1-78279-860-6 ebook: 978-1-78279-859-0

Most titles are published in paperback and as an ebook.
Paperbacks are available in traditional bookshops. Both print and
ebook formats are available online.
Follow us at:
https://www.facebook.com/ZeroBooks
https://twitter.com/Zer0Books
https://www.instagram.com/zero.books